UNDERSTANDING LYNN NOTTAGE

UNDERSTANDING CONTEMPORARY AMERICAN LITERATURE

Matthew J. Bruccoli, Founding Editor

Linda Wagner-Martin, Series Editor

Also of Interest

Understanding Alice Walker, Thadious M. Davis

Understanding Colson Whitehead, Derek C. Maus

Understanding David Mamet, Brenda Murphy

Understanding James Baldwin, Marc Dudley

Understanding James Grimsley, David Deutsch

Understanding John Edgar Wideman, D. Quinten Miller

Understanding Marsha Norman, Lisa Tyler

Understanding Randall Kenan, James A. Crank

Understanding Suzan-Lori Parks, Jennifer Larson

Understanding Tracy Letts, Thomas Fahy

UNDERSTANDING

LYNN NOTTAGE

Jennifer L. Hayes

THE UNIVERSITY OF SOUTH CAROLINA PRESS

Published by the University of South Carolina Press
Columbia, South Carolina 29208

uscpress.com

Printed in the United States of America

Library of Congress Cataloging-in-Publication Data
can be found at http://catalog.loc.gov/

ISBN: 978-1-64336-509-1 (hardcover)
ISBN: 978-1-64336-510-7 (paperback)
ISBN: 978-1-64336-511-4 (ebook)

For Mama (Regina L. Hinds)
I have always loved you and I aways will.

CONTENTS

SERIES EDITOR'S PREFACE

The Understanding Contemporary American Literature series was founded by the estimable Matthew J. Bruccoli (1931–2008), who envisioned these volumes as guides or companions for students as well as good nonacademic readers, a legacy that will continue as new volumes are developed to fill in gaps among the nearly one hundred series volumes published to date and to embrace a host of new writers only now making their marks on our literature.

As Professor Bruccoli explained in his preface to the volumes he edited, because much influential contemporary literature makes special demands, "the word *understanding* in the titles was chosen deliberately. Many willing readers lack an adequate understanding of how contemporary literature works; that is, of what the author is attempting to express and the means by which it is conveyed." Aimed at fostering this understanding of good literature and good writers, the criticism and analysis in the series provide instruction in how to read certain contemporary writers—explicating their material, language, structures, themes, and perspectives—and facilitate a more profitable experience of the works under discussion.

In the twenty-first century Professor Bruccoli's prescience gives us an avenue to publish expert critiques of significant contemporary American writing. The series continues to map the literary landscape and to provide both instruction and enjoyment. Future volumes will seek to introduce new voices alongside canonized favorites, to chronicle the changing literature of our times, and to remain, as Professor Bruccoli conceived, contemporary in the best sense of the word.

Linda Wagner-Martin, Series Editor

ACKNOWLEDGMENTS

I would like to thank a few people for their constant encouragement as I completed this project.

Dr. Claudia Barnett has proven an invaluable supporter of all my work. Thank you for your support.

Narja McElroy is the best friend an academic could have. Thank you for listening.

Finally, I thank Lilly and Daisy for your love and positivity.

CHAPTER 1

An Introduction to Lynn Nottage

In October 2022, Lynn Nottage lectured at the Pappas Visiting Artist Series at Stockton University. In her speech, she explained how her personal history impacts her writing. "My experience is very complicated, and diverse, and doesn't always adhere to the traditional paradigms. . . . As such, I'm really interested in creating theater that explores the cultural tensions inherent in being a Black woman living in this multicultural society that's still struggling very much with the painful legacy of racism and sexism. I toy with popular assumptions about race and gender with hopes of arriving at an entirely fresh perspective. Subverting expectations is part of my artistic mission."[1] Lynn Nottage is the only female playwright to win two Pulitzer Prizes for drama. That honor connects her with fellow playwrights Tennessee Williams and August Wilson. She accomplished this achievement first with *Ruined* (2009) and then with *Sweat* (2015). Already critically lauded, Nottage reached new heights of popularity in 2022 when she became the most produced playwright in the United States.

Describing her approach to writing her 2016 Pulitzer Prize award–winning play *Sweat*, Nottage claims that she chose to "replace judgment with curiosity."[2] Nottage's authorial curiosity stems from her upbringing. Her perspective was shaped by her home. Currently, "Nottage lives in the house where she grew up, a century-old brownstone on Dean Street, in Boerum Hill, Brooklyn, filled with modern art and African masks collected by her parents, Ruby and Wally Nottage."[3] Nottage's parents, a social worker and public school teacher, purchased the home in 1966 and incorporated aspects of Afrocentric education into their home life.[4] Although the community is now gentrified like many other Brooklyn neighborhoods, when Nottage was a child, the diversity of working-class people who lived there made an impression on her. Her community comprised various people from different backgrounds. Although she notes that just blocks away, streets were segregated by ethnicity, Nottage enjoyed the privilege of interacting with neighbors of various backgrounds on her block. Her home normalized diversity and shaped her understanding of racial and ethnic difference; this perspective opened her up to the dynamic exchange between community members.

Nottage notes that the theater can present the world in simplistic terms by focusing on a narrow group of people. A part of her artistic agenda is to "open up a new conversation with audiences, offer them a view of our culture that folks don't often see on the stage."[5] Nottage accomplishes this goal and much more across her significant body of work. Her works include multicultural communities that investigate the tensions that arise as people struggle to live during complex periods.

POOF! and the Beginning of a Career

Nottage attended the High School of Music & Art in Lower Manhattan. After her graduation, she attended Brown University and earned a master's degree in fine arts at Yale University in playwriting. Despite her prestigious academic pedigree, she did not immediately enter the world of the stage after graduation. Instead, she took a position at Amnesty International as a press officer.[6] It was her experience serving at Amnesty International that provided a catalyst for her to combine playwriting with politics. While working, she saw various images of victims of domestic abuse. However, Amnesty International did not have a process for addressing this specific problem. Her job did not provide an avenue to respond to the problem; therefore, Nottage turned to playwriting to do so. As she describes it, "I was so incredibly moved to respond immediately. And so I looked at these images and went into my office and *Poof!* came out of that."[7] Nottage's experience with Amnesty International allowed her to combine various elements of her education. Before this moment, she was a writer, but during this early stage of her life, she "felt as though she [didn't] have anything to write about."[8] Her craft was born from a desire to address social issues. After composing *POOF!*, Nottage entered it into a ten-minute play competition sponsored by the Actors Theatre of Louisville. She won that competition and began to pursue a professional career as a playwright.

The premise for *POOF!* is surprisingly humorous, given the serious subject matter at the core of the play. The tersely written play explores the significance of domestic violence in the life of Loureen. Loureen is portrayed as a sympathetic figure struggling to grapple with the supernatural conclusion to a very common problem. Key to Loureen's survival in an unhappy marriage has been her relationship with her neighbor and best friend, Florence. Nottage incorporates a community of women within the text to emphasize the importance of support for survival. As Florence tries to understand what has happened, Loureen explains, "he was shouting like he does, being all colored, then he raised up that big crusty hand to hit me, and poof, he was gone. . . . I barely got words out and I'm looking down at a pile of ash."[9] The shocking conclusion of Samuel's life is unbelievable, primarily because of the ordinary nature of his crime. Samuel has a reputation for harming Loureen and, despite calls to the police, nothing has changed his behavior until Loureen uses her voice.

POOF! laid the groundwork for a robust career. In total, Nottage has composed eleven full-length plays: *Crumbs from the Table of Joy*; *Por'Knockers*; *Mud, River, Stone*; *Las Meninas*; *Intimate Apparel*; *Fabulation*; *Ruined*; *By the Way, Meet Vera Stark*; *Sweat*; *Mlima's Tale*; and *Clyde's*. In addition to her full-length plays, she has published three 10-minute plays and has shifted toward musical theater, crafting the book for the highly successful *MJ the Musical* and *The Secret Lives of Bees*, as well as writing the libretto for the operatic adaptation of *Intimate Apparel*. Nottage's contributions to the theater are expansive, and her recent productions hint at a growing desire to incorporate music into her repertoire. Nottage's appeal stems from her ability to foreground human relationships within her texts. Starting with *Poof!*, she establishes an ability for tackling the pervasive issues that plague society by foregrounding the individuals in the center of the fray. Her commitment to crafting nuanced depictions of people who face pressing problems provides a strategy for examining her works.

However, Nottage's work is not limited to the stage. In addition to her plays, Nottage cofounded Market Road Films with her husband, Tony Gerber. Through Market Road Films, Nottage has been able to support documentary films, podcasts, and performance art pieces. Notably, an art installation titled *This Is Reading* tackled the issues of poverty and deindustrialization in America's former industrial cities. This work accompanied her play *Sweat*. Additionally, her producing and writing skills were utilized for the Netflix drama *She's Gotta Have It*, adapted from Spike Lee's 1986 film of the same name, for which she wrote the third episode of the first season, titled "#LBD (Little Black Dress)." Her foray into media serves as a natural progression of her use of multimodal forms in her full-length plays. For example, in *Crumbs from the Table of Joy*, Nottage blends elements of film into her play. Her commitment to multimodal performance strategies shows her ability to bend the boundaries of the stage by crafting dynamic pieces that reach a wide audience.

The American stage has long been a place that presents a narrow impression of experiences. In this contemporary moment where women and minority writers continue to be less produced, Lynn Nottage's success challenges the norm. Nottage's body of work takes an extensive look at the lives of Black women in the United States and globally. Her commitment to utilizing the stage as a place for political conversations about the experiences of marginalized women began with *Poof!* and continues in her most recent works. She has used the stage to tell innovative stories by focusing on people who are often pushed aside. Additionally, Nottage's popular and critical success challenge what Brandi Wilkins Cantonese calls "commonly held assumptions that supporting the work of women playwrights is an unwelcome economic risk, and that in time, both Nottage and the playwrights who come after her will benefit from that challenge to conventional wisdom."[10] Her marketability is an important step to opening up space for future playwrights to populate the stage with a variety of experiences that express the complex narratives about an ever-changing dynamic global population.

Nottage's plays investigate several topics. Sandra Shannon notes that "despite the distinct nature of Nottage's individual plays, each tends to focus upon one or more of the playwright's reoccurring themes: rescuing voices from history; discovering silencing between the lines; Black women defining themselves; race, multiculturalism, and diversity; escaping reality."[11] Nottage has a knack for historicizing marginalized people's perspectives about important topics and is adept at approaching political subject matter in a pragmatic way that does not convey a didactic approach but instead focuses on humanizing people grappling with complex problems. Nottage emphasizes people while considering their political context. Consequently, Nottage should be read as a writer deeply devoted to humanizing characters and providing them the stage as a space to finally be heard.

In *Understanding Lynn Nottage*, I examine the people at the heart of Nottage's works. As noted earlier, she is a writer who is keenly aware of differences because of her upbringing in a multicultural Brooklyn neighborhood. From that vantage, she crafts dynamic narratives that bring diverse perspectives together. Within her works, she tackles historical and contemporary issues without sounding preachy or judging her subjects. Instead, Nottage focuses on average people and acknowledges their humanity despite their flaws or strengths. In her interview with Dominic Maxwell for *The Times*, Nottage states "I'm drawn to telling stories I don't see. And I think for a really long time you didn't see accurate representations of working-class people on the stage. If you saw them they were people who were loud and bombastic but you didn't see the complexities of what people were going through.[12] Nottage encourages audiences to see the humanity in her characters, whether they are a southern Black male transplant to New York City who gets swept up in a cult or a 1930s African-American actress dreaming of starring in a feature film.

The book is organized chronologically, examining each full-length manuscript by Nottage to highlight the specific political issue and community she foregrounds. This organizational strategy emphasizes Nottage's commitment to privileging stories and characters that audience's traditionally do not witness on stage by connecting their personal narratives to the political situations that surround them. In chapter 2, "Migration in *Crumbs from the Table of Joy*," I explore the Crumps's journey during the second wave of the Great Migration as a personal quest resulting from grief of the loss of the family's matriarch. In chapter 3, "Humanizing Terror on the Stage in *Por'Knockers* and *Mud, River, Stone*," I focus on Nottage's evaluation of domestic terrorism, which consistently humanizes characters instead of reducing them to victims or aggressors. I argue in chapter 4, "Reclaiming a Voice from the Past in *Las Meninas*," that Nottage examines the role of perspective within art and uses the image of the Black Nun of Moret for a discussion that emphasizes that historical accounts require multiple perspectives to understand the complexity of an event or person. In chapter 5, "Marriage and Respectability in *Intimate Apparel* and *Fabulation*," I compare Nottage's investigations of respectability politics for two very different Black female entrepreneurs. In chapter 6, "Sexual Trauma and Survival in *Ruined*," I question what survival means during armed conflict. Chapter 7, "Humanizing Performers in *By the Way, Meet Vera Stark*," discusses representation of race in various media forms and how film has contributed to distorted images of Blackness. In chapter 8, "Anticipating the Political Divide in *Sweat*," I explore the economic policies that led to the recession of 2008 and anticipated the political divide in the United States by examining the lives of hardworking Americans. In chapter 9, "The Question of Values in *Mlima's Tale*," I analyze the connection between the exploitation of wildlife and their habitats with poaching. Finally, in the conclusion, "The Future Is Nottage and Elusive Justice in *Clyde's*," I evaluate Nottage's most recent full-length play, *Clyde's*, as an evaluation of the prison industrial complex while considering Nottage's legacy.

Nottage consistently shifts marginalized voices from the fringes to the center of global discussions. From victims of domestic abuse to a forgotten Black princess, Nottage provides a space on the stage for forgotten individuals to be heard. That is the power of Nottage's work. She uses her prowess as a writer to contextualize social issues while humanizing characters. The tone of her works, while political, is rarely didactic. Instead, she affords a space for the audience to draw their own conclusions by listening to the experiences of women and men whose voices are rarely heard. Her ability to refrain from judgment allows her to use the stage as a platform for providing silenced voices an opportunity to speak. She enters various historical eras and exhumes voices from the shadows. As her literary corpus continues to grow, Nottage is sure to remain a central dramatic voice examining social problems while humanizing communities of people who struggle to balance their values with shifting societal norms.

CHAPTER 2

Migration in *Crumbs from the Table of Joy*

Crumbs from the Table of Joy (*Crumbs*) premiered off-Broadway at the Second Stage Theatre in May 1995 as a part of a teen audience initiative. Directed by Joe Morto, the cast included Kisha Howard, Nicole Leach, Daryl Edwards, Ella Joyce, and Stephanie Roth. Set in 1950 in Brooklyn, *Crumbs* follows the Crump family, which includes father, Godfrey, and children, Ermina and Ernestine, after their relocation from Pensacola, Florida, to Brooklyn, New York. After the death of the teenage girls' beloved mother, Sandra, her sister Lily Ann arrives, supposedly to offer them a feminine influence. Nottage explores a family's individual migration within the larger context of the historical exodus of African Americans from the south to the north known as the Great Migration. There were multiple waves of the Great Migration. The Crump family transitioned during the second wave. Laurie Lanzen Harris states that "from 1940–1970, a Second Great Migration occurred in the United States . . . African American populations expanded throughout much of the country, and black migrants climbed economic and social ladders to enter the middle class by the millions. They also became a potent political force during this period. Confronted by continued discrimination and racism, African Americans launched a national fight for freedom and equality that culminated with the civil rights movement."[1]

Historically, the oppressive hold of southern Jim Crow laws on African-American people diminished their quality of life and provided a catalyst for their movement north. Although many African Americans left the South looking for more economic opportunity and social mobility, the impetus for the Crumps's move concerns the death of their matriarch: "Death brought us to

Brooklyn, the Nostrand Avenue stop on the A line. . . . A basement apartment, kind of romantic, like a Parisian artist's flat."[2] Nottage incorporates elements of southern disparities while emphasizing the desire for personal growth. Within this familial play, Nottage presents migration as a quest for sanctuary, yet this promise remains out of reach for the Crumps in the North as it had been in the South.

Nottage shows how movement from the South to the North provides the Crumps with the opportunity to develop beyond the confines of the South's rigid racial order. This is most evident through Ernestine, as her perspective shapes the narrative of the work. Throughout *Crumbs*, Ernestine frames the family's narrative as a struggle with change. Each character grapples with the transformation in their surroundings as a result of their journey and the loss of their matriarch. The past represented by the family's life in Florida is framed by grief, and their move offers an opportunity for healing. "Something better is always on the horizon."[3] Sandra Crump's death literally transforms the structure of the family and results in an omnipresent absence. In their basement apartment in Brooklyn, "on the mantle is a photograph of Sandra Crump . . . smiling gloriously."[4] The center of the familial home, the hearth, revolves around Sandra's memory and shapes the family's present reality as each family member responds to their grief.

Nottage connects the specific loss the family suffers to the cultural loss that thousands of African Americans experienced because of the Great Migration. Migration narratives within African-American literature dramatize the personal challenges Black people faced in their quest for civil liberties. Isabel Wilkerson argues that the Great Migration "grew out of the unmet promises made after the Civil War and, through the sheer weight of it, helped push the country toward the revolutions of the 1960s."[5] This historical era presented an opportunity for African Americans to demonstrate agency over their lives.

Although southern African Americans ventured north to avoid oppressive conditions in the South, others left to find work in industrial centers. Farah Jasmin Griffith contends that "most migration narratives offer a catalyst for leaving the south. Although there are different reasons for migrating, in all cases the south is portrayed as an immediate, identifiable, and oppressive power."[6] The combined economic and social motivations prompted "all totaled, between 1900–1970, some six million black men and women fled the Southern states."[7] Lawrence R. Rodgers posits that "the basic drive for migration is the search for a livable home. Because who one is relies on possessing a sense of one's place in the world . . . the process of migration is indelibly tied into the broader quest for identity."[8] Nottage's portrayal of the Great Migration foregrounds a journey toward healing. Sandra Crump's life is enmeshed with Florida and symbolizes loss. Godfrey Crump's decision to move to the North initially does not reflect the motivations of other Black migrants of his time. However, his view of New York resembles other migrants' romantic visions of New York. As the Crumps move forward, they face an uncertain future without a community to help them process the loss or establish new roots in their chosen home.

Migrants brought their cuisine, heritage, and cultural expressions to the North, but the important connections to their communities in the South were detrimentally impacted by their departure. Playwright August Wilson characterized the Great Migration as a mistake for African-American people: "We uprooted ourselves and attempted to transplant this culture to the pavements of the industrialized north. And it was a transplant that did not take."[9] Sandra Shannon contends that Wilson's "characters are often portrayed as wide-eyed optimists who, despite their earnest attempts to determine their destinies, either perish in the city or become part of its human refuse."[10] Wilson's analysis of the loss that African Americans experienced through the Great Migration affords little opportunity for reconciliation of the cultural richness of the South with the social opportunity of the North. Wilson promotes a return to the agrarian South that idealizes the community while negating the pain experienced by the migrants in their native lands. I argue that, in *Crumbs*, Nottage examines loss individually and communally through the Crumps's journey to the North. Nottage's contribution to migration narratives is her inclusion of a return to the South. Ernestine's and Ermina's development is not contingent upon attaining success in the North; rather, their ability to synthesize their experiences in the North and South affords them an opportunity to continue their journeys, which represents a possibility for restoration by moving forward.

Godfrey's Quest for Peace

Godfrey Crump's journey from Pensacola to Brooklyn is guided by hope. The grief he experiences after the death of his wife overwhelms him, and his desire for healing leads him to reach out to an unlikely source. Ernestine recalls, "Daddy discovered Father Divine when he was searching to cure 'the ailments of the heart,' those terrible fits of mourning that set in. Father Divine, the great provider, sent his blessing via mail. And shortly thereafter Daddy was cured."[11] Courtney Stars notes the historical figure Father Divine: "This letter from the Library of Congress regards a man who probably began his life named George Baker. He may have been born in a shanty house built on the red Georgia clay as the son of ex-slaves, or possibly he came from the bustling city neighborhood in Rockville, Maryland known disparagingly as 'Monkey Row.' At the end of his life, however, he was known as Father Divine. He claimed to be God, and scores of others believed it too."[12]

Nottage connects the postwar era to the antebellum period in African-American literature through the presentation of the North as divine. Father Divine, much like New York City, represents a supernatural solution for real-world problems. Godfrey's experience in the South is colored by pain. By shifting locales, he believes that he will physically distance himself from the negative experiences endured in Florida. However, migrants from the antebellum period, reconstruction, and the early twentieth century realized that issues of race in the United States were not centralized to one region of the country. Instead, migrants discovered that the problems from which they fled were also present in the promised land of the North. Nottage dramatizes this disillusionment through Godfrey's first disappointment: "He vowed to move nearer to Divine, to be close to God, devote his waking hours to the righteousness 'Divinely' ordained. Daddy thought Divine's Peace Mission was in Brooklyn, 'cause of a return address on a miracle elixir boasting to induce 'peace of mind.' Divine was not in Brooklyn or New York City."[13] Father Divine's absence from New York foreshadows the elusive nature of freedom for African Americans in the United States. Godfrey experiences racial tensions in his new home and still feels the overwhelming loss of his wife. Consequently, New York poses new problems that Godfrey seeks to solve through his devotion to Father Divine and his Peace Mission.

By following his religious leader's example, Godfrey attempts to transform his reality. In act I, scene I, Godfrey anxiously awaits the *New Day*, a periodical published by Father Divine and mailed to his congregants. The newsletter directs his disciples to worship Father in specific ways, including donating money and possessions to the Peace Mission. Godfrey believes that, through acts of devotion, he can change his destiny and achieve peace. His faith is guided by revisionist action. One example of this behavior is the adoption of new names for the family. "ALERT! I have considered your request and decided to bestow upon one of my devoted disciples beautiful names for your family. Names that God will immediately recognize and open up a direct line of communication. All that said and done, I give you the names Godfrey Goodness. . . . For your eldest, Darling Angel. And your baby, Devout Mary."[14] Godfrey welcomes his family's new names as a sign of prosperity through his inclusion into a religious community. The names bestowed by Father Divine signal a metaphorical new day that heightens his expectation of positive change connected to his journey from Florida to New York, but his reliance on Father

Divine exhibits his continued disempowered position. However, for Godfrey, this symbolic gesture underscored a new direction in their lives. Godfrey partially continues the quest for freedom with his journey to New York; however, he accepts a new name from Father Divine that shifts his agency to another source. Godfrey's discipleship manifests as submission, as he adopts the creed of the Peace Mission. He takes it a step further by modeling aspects of his personal life after Father Divine.

Father Divine's seemingly absolute power over his followers resulted in his reputation as a cult leader. However, Jill Watts rejects this label arguing that "American society has historically relegated many African-American religious movements to marginal status, the label robs credibility from the creation and development of black theological alternatives."[15] Although there are certainly issues of control within this religious sect, the Peace Missions fulfill a positive promise to the followers. The organization sought to uplift members through positive self-talk that would spiritually transform their negative situations into positive realities. Watts states, "he clearly taught his disciples to believe that he was God," Father Divine also encouraged his followers to consider how their own language could alter their realities.[16] This empowered mindset was meant to connect the members to his power and afford them an opportunity to channel "his spirit for material and spiritual success."[17] Although the Crumps arrive in New York in 1950, seeking a new way of life that is different from the restrictive Jim Crow South, Godfrey willingly adopts an alternative restrictive lifestyle in the hopes of changing his family's outcome. Godfrey adopts the language of Father Divine from the *New Day* periodicals, but there are still questions that he wrestles to understand in his new environment.

> Lily: What do you keep writing down?
> Godfrey: Oh, nothing, just questions. Things I want to ask Father Divine when he comes to New York for the Holy Communion.[18]

The opportunity to receive answers from God never comes. Nevertheless, Godfrey does not lose hope in Father Divine. The questions represent unanswered prayers to God and evidence his continued devotion to his faith. Godfrey's belief does not waiver despite his unanswered pleas; instead, he continues to emulate his leader's behavior in hopes to achieve the peace he so desperately seeks.

In act 1, scene 5, Godfrey suddenly marries Gerte, a German immigrant. His decision represents an attempt to manifest divine change within his home life. As the girls continue to mature, Godfrey turns to Father Divine for guidance in their rearing. Initially, when Lily arrives to their Brooklyn apartment, she claims, "I promised Nana I'd look after these girls for her. She don't think its proper that a man be living alone with his daughters once they sprung bosom."[19] Lily's rationale speaks to a conservative tradition to which she does adhere. Her true desire is for shelter and to be close to family. Her presence and allusion to the girls' maturity creates tension within the household that Godfrey attempts to rectify by marrying Gerte. Godfrey had a model for marrying a White woman in Father Divine. Unlike his leader, Godfrey does not belong to a social class that affords him protection from racial prejudice in his everyday life. Of the historical Father Divine, Kenneth E Burnham explains, "Father Divine was married to a blond Canadian follower, Edna Rose Ritchings. He explained that she was a reincarnation of his first wife, Peninah, who had become dissatisfied with her large, heavily body form. He had finally let her "pass," after years during which she had asked for that privilege. . . . Father Divine made it very clear that this was a symbolic marriage, never to be consummated in the worldly physical sense."[20] Father Divine married Ritchings in 1946. His insular environment and extreme wealth afforded him distance from people outside of the Peace Mission. Godfrey's home in Brooklyn does not provide him the same sanctuary, nor does he experience peace within his home because of his new union. By marrying Gerte, Godfrey signals to Lily Ann that she is no longer needed, which results in Lily's descent into alcoholism. Ernestine and Ermina are equally alienated by their father's decision, because it creates tension for them at school and with their neighbors. Additionally, Godfrey's marriage is met with a violent reaction when a group of angry White men attack him.[21] Godfrey did not anticipate this response and is left distraught. Ultimately, he turns back to Father Divine for guidance with prayers. Despite the negative reactions from his family and members of the community, Godfrey decides to stay committed to her and follow Father Divine's model for self-improvement.

Godfrey's actions throughout the play demonstrate his desperation for change. After the death of his beloved wife, religion plays a role in soothing his grief. As a result, his devotion to Father Divine motivates his movement north. Godfrey faces issues with racism and discrimination in the North and is physically assaulted because of his interracial marriage, yet, he never loses faith. His despair transforms into an undying resolve to alter his physical reality through spiritual practice. He is no longer drowning in grief, but the social issues that plague his family remain, because his new religious dedication does not transform his social reality. The positivity that he gains from following Father Divine improves his outlook on his circumstances. Although racism and bigotry remain ever present, Godfrey has transformed from a discouraged man to an optimistic father and husband who expects good things to happen in his life.

Lily's Personal Revolution

Lily embodies the setbacks to the Great Migration. Her inability to attain meaningful success in the North results in her radicalization. Claudia Jones reflects the frustrations of African-American women who exited the South for better social opportunities and joined political organizations only to find that many of the liberal movements were tainted with racist and sexist biases, in her 1949 essay "An End to the Neglect of the Problems of the Negro Woman!" Jones observes:

> An outstanding feature of the present stage of the Negro liberation movement is the growth in the militant participation of Negro women in all aspects of the struggle for peace, civil rights, and economic security. Symptomatic of this new militancy is the fact that Negro women have become symbols of many present-day struggles of the Negro people. This growth of militancy among Negro women has profound meaning, both for the Negro liberation movement and for the emerging antifascist, anti-imperialist coalition.
>
> To understand this militancy correctly, to deepen and extend the role of Negro women in the struggle for peace and for all interests of the working class and the Negro people, means primarily to overcome the gross neglect of the special problems of Negro women. This neglect has too long permeated the ranks of the labor movement generally, of Left-progressives, and also of the Communist Party.[22]

Jones's commentary reflects Lily's perspective regarding political action and the drawbacks that Black women faced when participating in progressive movements.

Lily's trials in the South drove her to the North, but the North did not fulfill the promises of equal treatment. Toward the end of the play, Lily reveals to Ernestine what drove her North. "It was the year the white folk had burned out old Johnston, and we'd gathered at Reverend Duckett's church, listening to him preach on the evils of Jim Crow for the umpteenth time. . . . A few miscalculated words, not knowing I was intended to remain silent. You know what a miscalculation is? It's saying, 'If y'all peasy-head Negroes ain't happy, why don't you go up to city hall and demand some respect. I'm tired of praying goddamnit!'"[23] Lily's outburst in church changes her role within the community. She notes that both White and Black people alike shunned her for speaking out and not understanding her place in society. Her inability to remain silent in the face of injustices within the Black community reflects her defiant stance. However, the limited power Black women possessed in the early twentieth century prevented her from manifesting meaningful change at home. This treatment drove her north in search of like-minded warriors invested in transforming society through political revolution. She lands in Harlem and soon loses contact with her family. For Black communists in the early twentieth century, Harlem represented the perfect launching pad for political change. According to Earl Hutchinson, "the Communists in 1934 regarded Harlem as their stronghold. The Party's unemployment, tenant, and relief organizations had organized angry Harlemites in dozens of street demonstrations and mass rallies. The Party now had supporters in Harlem churches and civic and social organizations."[24] Lily's destination is purposeful. Harlem before World War II symbolized a Black cultural center where intelligent men and women came together to exchange ideas and revel in a community that promoted racial pride and uplift.

Lily embraces this progressive environment and encourages her nieces to think for themselves. However, her ideology creates tension within the family and with Godfrey. For example, Ernestine writes a school paper titled "The Colored Worker in the United States," which draws the ire of the principal, who scolds Godfrey about Ernestine's political ideas.[25] This clash at school continues at home and culminates in a screaming match between Godfrey and Lily over the children's education.

> Godfrey: She gonna apologize! And I'm going to tell you once, then I'm gonna leave it alone: we were doing just fine without your sorta learning. We don't want and we don't need it.
>
> Lily: Well, I promised mama I'd look after these babies. They need a woman's voice in this house, that's what they need.
>
> Godfrey: Maybe you ain't the right woman.[26]

This explosive argument represents Godfrey's and Lily's clashing ideologies. They both fled the South in hopes of finding sanctuary. However, the reality of New York encourages both to rely on outside forces for strength. Godfrey demonstrates a growing distrust of Communism and fears retribution. Mark Solomon asserts that "many blacks viewed Communists as pariahs who would only add to their already substantial vulnerability."[27] Godfrey's anger stems from his fear for his reputation and the safety of his children. Although he adheres to Father Divine's doctrine, he is aware of the real challenges that face Black people in the North and South. For Godfrey, Lily's intrusion into his family with her progressive ideas challenges the stability he feels through his religious practice. Conversely, Lily's political beliefs express her dissatisfaction with her social status. Her lessons to the children are meant to prepare them for the perilous environment beyond the safety of their home. However, Lily does not have a home of her own and is beholden to Godfrey. Her position within the Crump household is unstable. As a single Black woman in the 1950s, she occupies a fraught space, because she has not fulfilled heteronormative expectations. Her independent perspective is challenged by her reliance on Godfrey for shelter. She disagrees with him, but she is also attracted to the provision he symbolizes.

Ultimately, Lily is unable to create real change in New York City. Her failure is apparent from the moment she arrives at the family's door. She is homeless and without direction. Her time with the family exposes the obstacles she faces in the North. Robin D. G. Kelley has questioned the role of Black women in progressive political spaces: "What is the vision of women in Black radical visions of freedom. . . . They have never been a primary subject of the American Left, always falling somewhere in the cracks between the Negro question and the Woman question."[28] In Florida, Lily articulated her frustrations with her community regarding their limited response to problems with Jim Crow. She continues her defiance in New York City, but the results remain the same. She consistently finds little appreciation for her perspectives. Her inability to find a sanctuary signals the failure of communism to fully address the intersection of issues that racism, sexism, and classism present for Black women.

Lily's place in the home is usurped by Gerte. Once Godfrey remarries, Lily's initial justification for their living arrangement is no longer necessary. Consequently, she begins to drink incessantly, devolving into alcoholism. Lily's reliance on alcohol foreshadows her journey's conclusion. While purposeful, her journey has not created meaningful change in her life. She feels unwanted, and the problems that she left behind have followed her to New York. Ever proud, she refuses to acknowledge defeat and instead withdraws from the family. "Well . . . actually, Ernie, I . . . I have been invited to a conference in upstate New York, Albany area. I been meaning to tell you. (Continues to toy with the bottle) They want me to lecture or something like that. They've recognized that I'm an expert on the plight of the Negro woman. I've been thinking about going."[29] Her withdrawal from the family represents a final defeat in her quest for sanctuary. She has been unable to find a space where she feels free to express her perspective. Nottage uses Lily's narrative to highlight the systematic oppression that African-American women face in the United States. Within and beyond the African-American community, African-American women are pressured to occupy a supportive role within the household. Within the domestic space, they lack a safe space to articulate the issues that they personally face, because their purpose is to uplift their partners and children. Although their position is to support, they receive little support from others. Lily decides not to marry or have children. As a result, she dwells in the margins of her community. Despite this harsh reality, Lily's final action within the play is to encourage Ernestine to establish a space for herself beyond the revolution. "You want to be part of my revolution? You know what I say to that, get yourself a profession like a nurse or something so no matter where you are or what they say, you can always walk into a room with your head held high, 'cause you'll always be essential."[30]

Lily empowers Ernestine by encouraging her to apply the lessons she has learned during her journey. While Lily might not have found a space to call home, she has not lost hope because she foresees a future for her niece. Instead of encouraging Ernestine to follow in her footsteps, Lily encourages her to carve out an independent path while establishing a safety net that would allow her to stand outside of the patriarchal expectation of marriage while also contributing a useful skill to the community. Lily's lesson suggests that African-American women's value is contingent on the work they accomplish for others. Thus, their survival is reliant on their ability to demonstrate their usefulness in the home and in the community.

Ernestine's Journey Home

Ernestine Crump's perspective directs the movement within *Crumbs*. Because she is the narrator, her impressions of the tensions within the family take center stage. Ernestine is only seventeen years old. This moment in her life is embedded with transition. Symbolically, Ernestine embodies the long civil rights movement. In the contemporary period, discussions of the civil rights movement does not consistently reflect the scope of the era. Instead of focusing on the period as a decades-long quest for civil rights, Jacquelyn Dowd Hall examines the movement as an ongoing struggle for equality that includes moments of progression and regressive response. She states,

> centering on what Bayard Rustin in 1965 called the 'classical' phase of the struggle, the dominant narrative chronicles a short civil rights movement that begins with the 1954 *Brown v. Board of Education* decision, proceeds through public protests, and culminates with the passage of the Civil Rights Act of 1964 and the Voting Rights Act of 1965. Then comes the decline. After a season of moral clarity, the country is beset by the Vietnam War, urban riots, and reaction against the excesses of the late 1960s and the 1970s, understood variously as student rebellion, black militancy, feminism, busing, affirmative action, or an overweening welfare state.[31]

Ernestine's journey in the play embodies the long civil rights movement. She is a character that embodies the possibilities of the second wave of the Great Migration, yet the struggles she experiences in New York City emphasize that progress does not happen quickly.

In addition to the family's movement from Florida to New York, she also grapples with the changes that her age brings. Throughout the play, Ernestine is focused on her graduation. Specifically, she is consumed with the creation of her graduation dress. Ermina reflects on the dress in act 1: "Mommy promised Ernie a graduation dress and she gonna need money for the fabric."[32] At the time of the declaration, Godfrey seems unaware of his daughter's progress, largely because his grief has made him insular. His focus has been primarily on his own pain. Although he considers the move to New York an opportunity for both of his daughters, he does not spend much time considering how the transition has impacted their lives. The focus on the graduation momentarily shifts Godfrey's perspective from himself to his children. The graduation dress embodies a promise for the past and the future. For Ernestine, the dress symbolizes her progression, and it represents her mother's commitment to her growth. Ernestine's impending graduation signals a turning point in her life when she will have to make meaningful choices about her direction.

During this moment of transition, Ernestine grapples with two different perspectives that shape her reality. Godfrey and Lily both function as teachers for Ernestine and embody distinctive ideologies regarding strategies for survival in New York:

> Godfrey: I keep telling you, I ain't that man. You insult my wife, you insult me. All' cause you got these big ideas about race and the world and we don't fit your picture. . . . And now you got my children taking up your lead.
>
> Lily: You say that with such contempt for me. I'm getting tired of you constantly berating me with your sanctified notions. I'm sorry for what happened to you and Gerte, but I will never apologize for who I am.[33]

Caught between her desires to please her father and to stay connected to her aunt, Ernestine learns from both. Ernestine represents the synthesis of her father's and her aunt's dreams. From Godfrey, she understands the importance of having values to guide your movement, but unlike her father, she possesses an inquisitive nature that prevents her from blindly following any singular ideology. Lily encourages Ernestine to be an independent thinker, and Ernestine benefits from the tutelage of both teachers. Her strength comes from her ability to consider multiple perspectives and apply lessons from each. Unlike

Godfrey and Lily, she does not view different perspectives as conflicting ideas. Her flexibility allows her to synthesize lessons from both figures by applying knowledge from their examples.

Ernestine invokes performance as a strategy to understand her complex homelife. Movies during the 1950s presented American values to their audience. These values counter the competing ideologies she experiences in her home. Nottage uses film in the play as a strategy for Ernestine to process the difficult scenes within her life by cinematically improving her reality. She manipulates her present when she feels unable to alter complex situations. The tensions between her father and Lily represent an intersection of values. To process this tension, Nottage frequently interrupts scenes with Ernestine's revisionist visualizations. For example, after Godfrey argues with Lily about his marriage to Gerte, Ernestine views the aftermath as a love scene from a 1950s film.

> Ernestine: (Suddenly, blue, flickering light engulfs Godfrey and Gerte, who kiss passionately, like film stars. A swell of music.) We'd recovered my father from Divine only to lose him to passion. The kiss. The transforming kiss that could solve all of their problems. Their kiss, a movie-time solution.[34]

Nottage uses elements from film to visualize Ernestine's attempts to make sense of competing perspectives. These moments in the play demonstrate Ernestine's internal conflict. Sometimes she revises the scene and substitutes an ending that she prefers when she feels powerless over the actions of others, but in this scene, she recognizes the problems within her father's marriage. She understands in this moment that the issues he faces remain; consequently, she imagines his joy in the moment as a substitute for addressing the violence he experienced in the street.

Ernestine's graduation signals the continuation of her journey. After graduating, she must decide how to move forward. Some options are reflective of the paths that Godfrey and Lily traveled before her.

> Godfrey: Down at the bakery they need another gal. One word from me and you're as good as in.
>
> Ernestine: Bakery? Imagine a life in the bakery by his side with no greater expectation than for the bread to rise. I don't know that that's what I want to do.
>
> Godfrey: I . . . I already told the folks at the bakery that you'd be working for them.
>
> Ernestine: You should have asked me, Daddy.

Godfrey: I don't see what the problem is. You have no job promised and nobody's knocking down this door to ask for your hand in marriage. I'm offering you something wonderful, Ernie.

Ernestine: But Daddy, I'm going to Harlem.

Godfrey: Forget about Lily, you follow her you know what you'll be taking on.[35]

Godfrey suggests that Ernestine has three possible paths. First, she could work with him at the bakery and continue living with the family. Second, she could marry. However, he callously suggests that this is not a reasonable option because of her lack of romantic interests. Finally, she could follow Lily to Harlem. This third option is mentioned curtly, which suggests his thoughts about her living an independent life. He acknowledges the difficulties that Lily faced and foresees a similar route for Ernestine should she decide to walk away from his home. However, Ernestine posits another option that her father neglects. She could pursue her education. Ernestine is not as disillusioned with the world as her Aunt Lily is. Additionally, she recognizes the limitations of adhering to the religious piety that Father Divine demands of his followers. Ernestine appreciates that her path forward will require her to chart a new direction if she is to move beyond her current position.

Continuing her education at City College provides Ernestine with a strategy for growth. She remains in New York as she extends her initial path from high school to the halls of higher education. This journey does not end in New York City. Instead, her education provides her with an opportunity to return to the south with the lessons she has learned in school and at home. In the epilogue, Ernestine reflects on her journey. "Years from now I'll remember my mother and the sweet-smelling humid afternoons by the Florida waters, and then years from now I'll ride the Freedom Bus back down home. . . ." Her path includes reflections of home and the application of lessons learned. Like Lily, Ernestine wants to change the world for the better. However, she does not lose her connection to her familial past as she attempts to move forward. Unlike Godfrey and Lily, Ernestine recognizes that her journey does not include one destination that represents an idealized endpoint. Survival requires consistent movement, both intellectual and physical. Ernestine's success is reflected through this progressive idea about travel. Instead of envisioning a future where her problems are resolved, she focuses on the present while "walking as far as these feet will take me. . . ."[36]

In *Crumbs*, Nottage considers the complex political reasons motivating migrants during the first wave of the Great Migration. Although many scholars note the socioeconomic motives influencing the exodus of Black migrants from the South, *Crumbs* establishes the Crumps's collective familial grief over the death of Sandra Crump as the key factor for their journey north. Nottage's approach creates a family drama within the era that reflects the issues of the time while focusing on the individual aspirations of Godfrey, Lily, and Ernestine.

CHAPTER 3

Humanizing Terror on the Stage in *Por'Knockers* and *Mud, River, Stone*

Nottage explores domestic terrorism in two works. However, the context and perpetrators of the acts have distinct agendas. Elyse Sommer states in her review of *Mud, River, Stone* that "Nottage explains the intriguing title of her new play as follows: 'Mud, river and stone are the basic elements of life and of civilization. They're what you use to build up a society, but they also can destroy it.'"[1] *Mud, River, Stone*, which premiered at Studio Arena Theatre in Buffalo, New York, in November 1996, directed by Seret Scott. includes a dynamic cast including Cheryl Turner, Marc Damon Johnson, Marcel Braithwaite, Ross Bickell, Mary F. Randle, Kevin Orton, and Drew Richardson. In *Mud, River, Stone,* a hostage situation is meant as an opportunity for restoration. On the other hand, the terrorist plot in *Por'Knockers* is an ideological act meant to send a message to the US government from a group of political zealots who are determined to make a statement about the ongoing destructive policies that the government enacts at home and abroad. Directed by Michael Rogers, *Por'Knockers* premiered at the Vineyard Theatre in November 1995 and featured a cast including Ray Ford, Afemo Omilami, Earl Nash, Sanaa Lathan, Ramon Melindez Moses, and Daniel Zelman.

The distinction is subtle, but Nottage ascribes a clear political ideology to the characters in *Por'Knockers* that frames their misguided attempt to rectify, in a singular act, centuries of colonial and imperial oppression against Black bodies globally. Although she faced little difficulty finding a venue to stage the work, the social circumstances beyond the production muddied the play's reception. In the interview, Nottage notes that during the initial workshop of the play at Dance Theater Workshop in September 1994, two key cultural milestones occurred: the Oklahoma City Bombing and the Million Man March.Nottage's description of the key issue in *Por'Knockers* extends to her following work, *Mud, River, Stone*, in which she uses humor again to characterize a tense political scene in a remote African resort when a hotel worker takes several people hostage because of his fear of impending war. This multicultural play questions the role that superpowers play in the lives of everyday men, women, and children.

Nottage uses humor and irony in both works to emphasize the fraught political spaces the characters occupy while simultaneously acknowledging the limited opportunities for change. Darryl Dickson-Carr suggests that "It is when African American satire utilizes the broad rhetorical trope of irony that it has the distinct advantage of being an excellent tool for those wishing to speak the otherwise unspeakable."[2] On the surface, the subject matter of both plays hardly seems funny. Yet, Nottage does incorporate humor to emphasize political issues that plague society. Rather than being solely a social satire, *Por'Knockers*, along with *Mud, River, Stone*, incorporates elements of irony and humor with social protest to explore the current moment. Incidents of domestic and international terrorism have shaped our society in destructive ways. Nottage's bold decision to go inside of the minds of "terrorists" to consider the ideologies that guide their destructive acts represents a specific desire to utilize the stage as a space to demystify global issues. By interrogating terror, Nottage moves beyond a social satire that uses wit to merely expose a problem. Although Nottage hesitates to label herself a political writer because "the label describes only one of my facets as a playwright," she does acknowledge that "the politics of omission" is pivotal in understanding her role as a playwright.[3] The stage offers artists an opportunity to enter into political discourse about pervasive issues. Her works avoid examining acts of terror in a bubble; instead, the plays function as an interrogation of the political landscape to more fully understand the symbolic meaning of the dramatic action that terrorists enact.

Por'Knockers explores domestic terrorism, whereas *Mud, River, Stone* considers the consequences of colonialism as reflected in former colonial properties in Africa. Both plays underscore the ways in which colonialism and capitalism combine to create complex scenarios in which people of color are exploited for their labor. As a result, both texts posit how Western nations consciously work to undermine the agency of minorities globally. Individuals who are fed up with this reality decide to take a stand, but the aftermath provides few positive results for those involved. This chapter demonstrates Nottage's exploration of the contemporary phenomenon of terrorism. I argue that both works consider how terrorism has become increasingly politicized, yet few are interested in the underlying situations that create terror. By unpacking the circumstances surrounding terrorist events, Nottage encourages her audience to consider the blowback that we experience reading about these sordid cases in the news. Nottage sheds light on diverse perspectives that are often left out of the political conversations about terrorism to offer her audience a space to reflect and heal.

Debating the Symbolism of the Domestic Terror in *Por'Knockers*

In *Por'Knockers*, Nottage centers a group of revolutionaries who plan and successfully commit an act of domestic terror. The group includes five key figures: Kwami, a Guyanese-American man who is the *de facto* leader of the group; Tamara, an African-American professor; James, an African-American man who struggles with paranoia; Ahmed, an African-American man in his twenties who displays a hypermasculine bravado; and Lewis, a Jewish-American man in his thirties. The group avoids using names when they gather at their meet-up point, a shabby apartment in Manhattan East New York City (NYC). Instead, they affect comradery through their costumes. By wearing similar blue suits, they visualize their unity and provide an air of sophistication to their political plot. The play is divided into eleven scenes that shift between the rainforest and the NYC apartment complex. The moments in the rainforest focus on a lone individual, Lance. The audience discovers that Lance is Kwami's father, who left his family several years before. The scenes with Lance counter the images between the revolutionaries. In Guyana, Lance is presented in solitude, panning for gold in a waterway, while Kwami's voice can be heard narrating Lance's action. The Guyanese scenes represent a counterpoint to the tense moments between the group as they consider their plans to wage war on governmental power structures. The humor within the play is established through these moments of tension.

In the beginning of the play, the group shifts into action to witness their destruction of the Federal Bureau of Investigation (FBI) building. It is clear that a plan had been made to attack the building on a state holiday to ensure that no one would be harmed. However, the group grapples with the reality of the act soon after it is completed. In scene 3, the group has reassembled except for one figure: James. The group waits for James to move onto the next part of the plan, which is taking responsibility for the act by calling federal agents and making their motives known to the government.

In the meantime, the group quarrels over the significance of the act they have taken. Ahmed, Kwami, and Lewis offer similar reactions connected to their respective ideas concerning masculinity. Ahmed's reaction reverberates with laughter and confidence. He questions boldly, "Did you see that shit? Did you hear it? Glass shattered everywhere, rained down like confetti. It was the joint."[4] Tamara challenges his jubilant response, calling the bombing and the destruction "a bit showy."[5] Before she can fully explain her reaction, Kwami counters that the bombing has a deeply symbolic meaning. "That building was an insult, an affront. We took it down, and nobody got hurt. That was the point."[6] His language in this moment is confident, but Kwami does not relish in this victory like Ahmed. He performs a more dignified jubilant reaction as he considers their act. Regardless, both Kwami and Ahmed are focused on the deeper meaning of striking out against the government. They are proud of their behavior because, to them, the building symbolized corruption. Thus, their action represents a movement to set things right. They have personalized their relationship, and Lewis continues to internalize the bombing as a personal message not just to the government but to his community: "Back home, no one would believe it. What do you think, Dad? Respect. Discipline. Fear. Oh no, we've joined the ranks. We'll be right up there in the pantheon, don't you think?"[7] Throughout *Por'Knockers*, Kwami is the character who most often references his father and seems guided by his idealized vision of this departed figure. However, in the direct aftermath of the bombing, Lewis considers how his father would perceive him as a man. In his mind, this act affirms not only his masculinity but also his passage into a collection of deified human beings who have stood up against injustice through violent means.

During their grandstanding, Tamara is the only person to consider the emptiness of their violent action. "Standing there. Being there. Watching, I thought the heavens would open and shower down some good grace. The rain threw me. I'd expected for a moment there would be some clarity, a vision through the broken glass and kerosene haze. I expected to hear some triumphal chorus arise. Not really, but you know what I'm saying. I guess I feel queasy. But, we succeeded. I suppose."[8] For Tamara, watching the destruction of the FBI building did not overwhelm her with a sense of power of joy. On the contrary, she expected more from this action but gains little insight. Although the men who were gathered see the destruction of the building as a response to grave wrongs facilitated by the government, their response seems hollow. In this moment, Tamara considers the conflict between her expectations and the reality of the scene she witnesses. She expected some confirmation of their deed from a divine power to steady her own belief that this act was necessary and righteous, but the explosion juxtaposed with the aftermath of the rain suggests a spiritual distance from God. In this moment, Nottage invokes aspects of religious extremism in Tamara's monologue to explore the connection that some terrorists believe exists between their destructive acts and divine providence. Notable political scientist Magnus Ranstorp explores various acts of terrorism from diverse religious practitioners and decides that "all are united in the belief on the part of the perpetrators that their actions were divinely sanctioned, even mandated, by God."[9] Tamara's sadness resonates from her realization that there was no divine affirmation of the bombing. Instead, she views the rain as a negative symbol, where the rain demonstrates God's ambivalence or disapproval. Either way, Tamara's reaction notes her dissatisfaction with her belief that their act was not divinely supported. In this scene, Nottage allows a moment for consideration about the nature of contemporary terrorist acts. Many acts are conducted by individuals who believe that they are guided by divine powers to alter the state of the world. Those who were indoctrinated in religious fundamentalist beliefs are misguided by their systems of faith and view the targets of their acts as collateral damage in a divine battle waged to appease their gods.

The members have eagerly awaited James's arrival to celebrate their victory, but his arrival transforms their celebration into a moment of regret.

> James: There were people in the building . . . children . . . I stayed behind and watched. The fire traveled like a terrible wind, without any consideration. I stood there, unable to move, to shout for help. I didn't know.
>
> Tamara: What happened?
>
> Ahmed: Yeah, and?
>
> James: A group of children, black kids, broke through the fence and were playing in the building. . . .[10]

After this revelation, the group considers the ramifications of their actions. They shift from a focus on the symbolism of the bombing to reflecting on the significance of the loss of life. Mark Juergensmeyer claims that there is a nature of destructive performance to acts of terror. He argues that the audience of terrorist acts should understand these demonstrative feats as "dramatic violence as part of a strategic plan. This viewpoint assumes that terrorism is always part of a political strategy—and, in fact, some social scientists have defined terrorism in just this way: 'the use of covert violence by a group for political ends.'"[11] One unique aspect of *Por'Knockers* is the group's mission to cause no physical harm to people. The bombing is meant as a symbolic strike against the government. However, their intentions are undermined by the reality of the children using their holiday to play in the building. The group envisions themselves as social justice warriors but that impression changes when they realize they have unwittingly murdered children.

The group's next step is to call a governmental office to take responsibility for the bombing. However, the discovery of victims changes the mood, and they now must regroup and decide what steps they should take. Whether they should accept responsibility is the conflict that drives the remaining action of the play. The tension within the group resembles the historical problems with sexism within Black nationalist organizations. Black women have consistently participated and organized within Black nationalist organizations. Within these same groups, men have undermined the importance of their participation. Michele Wallace notes that Stokely Carmichael once quipped that "the only position for women in SNCC is prone."[12] Wallace points to the sexist perception that some male members of revolutionary groups hold, that revolution starts with men and that women should function as supporters of this goal. Nottage subtly engages the hypocrisy within these organizations by focusing on Tamara's dissent. She is the lone voice that argues that the death of children is consequential and tarnishes the group's overarching goals. Her refusal to ignore the cost of liberation pushes the group to reconsider their core values.

In scene 7, before the group claims responsibility for their act, they descend into a philosophical question about the connection between their values and actions. Why do we need to make the call? What are we hoping our action will change? What do we want to happen as a result of the bombing? Unsurprisingly, the members have different responses for each question, despite the months of preparation that culminated in the bombing. Ahmed claims, "[W]e know what we want. We want emancipation, bang! We want freedom, boom! We want equality, bam!"[13] The problem is that their action has not moved them toward these goals. For Tamara, the death of the children places the group in opposition to the future they desire. Symbolically, the children represent the future that the group is fighting for, so if the bombing harms those whom it seeks to help, their goals seem untenable. The meeting continues to devolve as the disagreements over the significance of the victims of the bombing clouds the group's overarching goals. Ultimately, they agree to move forward with the call, but they have trouble finalizing a clear message to deliver to the authorities.

Tamara: The phone call.
Lewis: Let's just do it, let's just say we're a group of—
Ahmed: Black.
James: African-American—
Kwami: Diasporic people . . .
Lewis: Acting on the desire . . . to awaken this country to the persuasiveness of disaffection and alienation. It was—
Ahmed: is—
Kwami: was . . .

Lewis: . . . essential to grab the attention of the population by means of a bold and unfortunate act, but this is a society—

Tamara: Patriarchy.

James: Country.

Kwami: Eurocentric hegemony.

Ahmed: Place.

Lewis: "Culture" that responds to violence and therefore a violent act provides the path of least resistance to the psyche of this nation. . . . How's that?[14]

The group struggles to verbalize how their use of force connects with their intentions to change key issues in society. Although each member of the group craves change, they each harbor ambitions connected to their specific subject position. Their rush to act through the bombing has created a bottleneck of emotion as the group struggles to claim responsibility and acknowledge the death of the victims. Nottage incorporates humor throughout the discussion as the group disagrees about the wording of the call. Eventually, each character attempts to make the call, but they hang up before someone answers. Finally, Tamara makes the call and discovers that there is no one to answer because of the federal holiday; instead, her call is sent to voicemail, where she waits for an operator who never answers. The group incorrectly believes that they are in control of the circumstances of the bombing and the aftermath. However, every step they take to manifest control backfires. Nottage dramatizes the cycle of conflict that terrorist organizations respond to and simultaneously create. Although there are real systematic issues that plague any society, terrorist acts rarely create meaningful change.

Introduction to *Mud, River, Stone*

Nottage includes a note describing the inspiration for the play *Mud, River, Stone*. She read a short article from a 1994 edition of the *New York Times* that documented a hostage situation and the demands of the captors. "As I read on, what struck me most were the terrible scars left by the struggle, which would now take more than a generation to heal, for the people of Mozambique had been at war so long they did not know how to cope with peace."[15] The state of affairs in Mozambique reflects a former colonial state struggling to establish a clear path forward. Frantz Fanon states, "Decolonization, which sets out to change the order of the world, is clearly an agenda for total disorder. But it cannot be accomplished by the wave of a magic wand, a natural cataclysm, or a gentleman's agreement."[16] Nottage considers the consequences of colonial intervention into Africa in *Mud, River, Stone*.

A seemingly innocuous vacation transforms into a horrible memory. The play begins with a Black American couple, Sarah and David Bradley, recounting their vacation to Africa. As they tell their story, the scene shifts from a comfortable Manhattan apartment to the jungles of an unidentified southeastern African country. The memories come to life as the dinner party in the New York apartment disappears, and Sarah and David travel to the past. In essence, they reenact their experiences abroad. David recalls that "one of my friends had been to Africa a few years back, raved. He said it would change our lives. He said, if *he* had to do it all over again *he'd* go it alone, sans tour. See the continent without the filter. I thought it would be easier. You know, on us."[17] This reflection reveals some of the mistakes the couple made in their attempt to take a vacation to Africa. They were underprepared for their trip and viewed the expedition in a superficial way. Sarah remarks that David "wanted to see the continent, like the naturalists on the 'Discovery Channel.' . . . He wanted to see the mud and stone ruins of our ancestors."[18] David's desire to reclaim his connection to his African heritage connects to cultural and genealogy travel.

Within the African-American literary tradition, travel has been used as a vehicle to flee oppression. From slave narratives to the travel exploits of the expatriate writers, African-American writers have incorporated travel in their writings to expose the ways movement can be used as a protest strategy. Nottage uses travel differently in *Mud, River, Stone*. Her use of travel exposes the distance that Americans—including African Americans—have from the struggles that some African people face with the legacy of imperialist intervention. David and Sarah view travel as an opportunity to escape from the banalities of their middle-class work life. For them, travel to Africa represents an opportunity for cultural tourism. The Bradleys perform as cultural voyeurs who seek connection with the people of Africa without offering a meaningful exchange. As they travel deeper into southeastern Africa, away from approved tourist locations, the Bradleys are removed from safety. Their dream of reconnecting with their past is undercut when they make a wrong turn. Literally and symbolically, the Bradleys are lost in Africa. Once separated from the undemanding image of Africa, the Bradleys experience a war-torn village healing from decades of ongoing struggle. Sarah notes that the couple rented a car and drove past an unintelligible sign into the bush. After running out of gas, they are overwhelmed by a harsh rainstorm that sends them scrambling for cover. In the midst of their misfortune, they spot the Imperial Hotel.

Setting the Stage for an International Incident

The Imperial Hotel is the setting for an international incident. The memory that the Bradleys recount at a dinner party in Brooklyn is the entryway for the audience into a broader discussion of decolonialization. Initially, Nottage uses the Bradleys to initiate a conversation regarding the lingering impact of colonialism in Africa. Within the hotel, she includes the Bradleys to symbolize a disconnect from the African continent. Her depiction of African Americans emphasizes their first-world privilege and diminishes their connection to Africans living in developing countries. Initially, the Bradleys seem like the focus of the narrative, but the play truly focuses on two characters: Mr. Blake and Joaquim. The rain provides a catalyst for the characters to come together at the hotel, but it is the tension between Mr. Blake and Joaquim that creates the conflict that drives the action of the narrative. In act 1, Mr. Blake behaves like the proprietor of the hotel. He commands Joaquim to make his drink and he shapes the conversation within the hotel. His condescending attitude stems from his familial connection to the resort. Mr. Blake states:

> My uncle built it in the thirties. He had a vision of a railway from the coast cutting across the continent. He built this hotel not even by a river, hoping that he could bribe the officials to have the railway pass through here. . . . It was a splendid dream. Can you imagine the insanity that brokered this magnificence? The chandelier was brought up from South Africa. The wood, the finest mahogany, imported from West Africa. The glass, from Cairo. This hotel represents the totality of the continent. He thought he could bring it all together under one roof. Here now, the embodiment of an idea gone sour.[19]

His comments about the hotel reflect nostalgia for a colonial era long past. For Blake, the hotel imbodies the genius of the colonial agenda and echoes the problems that imperialism caused for local Africans. As he lists the components of the hotel, Nottage subtly interweaves past European intervention in the continent into the present moment of the play. The carving of Africa into parts for the consumption of its natural resources speaks to the plunder that Africa faced at the hands of European superpowers dating back to the nineteenth century at the Berlin Conference.[20] The commodification of Africa reduced the land and people to items ripe for exploitation. The results of this ideology reflect Mr. Blake's current attitude toward the hotel and the native community that populates the area. The legacy of wealth within Blake's family has afforded him opportunities that have been systematically denied to local Africans by the same institutions that support individuals like Blake's uncle. Ultimately, Mr. Blake's continued presence in central Africa suggests the lasting benefit of colonialism for White descendants of European colonists.

Joaquim serves as a counterpoint to Mr. Blake's perspective. He challenges Blake by providing a counternarrative that articulates a different point of view regarding the hotel: "He says his uncle built this hotel, but it is not the truth. Our village did. Look closely at the details throughout the rooms. You will see our history carved into the woodwork. Our stories are all there."[21] Blake claims ownership of the hotel and the materials that created the resort, but Joaquim disputes this assessment. The labor reflected in the craftsmanship of the hotel and the labor needed to transport materials across the continent represent colonized people's labor. In other words, Joaquim asserts that the work that built the vestiges of colonial power result from the efforts of African people. When Europeans claim ownership of the materials and the commodities built from colonized labor, they deny the legacy of Black craftsman and laborers whose blood and sweat account for products. Nottage uses Joaquim as a political symbol for disenfranchised Africans. She affords him an opportunity to acknowledge the toll that the exploitation of African resources and people continues to have in decolonized regions. The instability that resulted from colonial intervention in Africa allowed for the rise of unstable political regimes that followed Europe's departure from the continent.

The Hostage Situation

Nottage investigates the impact of decolonization on the descendants of colonists and the colonized in *Mud, River, Stone*. The characters in the play figuratively represent global interests in the conflict occurring in this mythic southeast African country. In addition to the Bradleys, two other characters visit the Imperial Hotel seeking assistance. The first is Ama Cyllah, who is described as a "West African aid worker, educated in England, late twenties."[22] Ama works at a nearby mission and has ventured to the hotel to use the telephone to request supplies. Nottage's inclusion of Ama in the play hints at a larger political message: Africa is not a monolith. Ama is Nigerian and has been educated. She uses her education to invest in underserved communities in Africa. However, Ama is not a fully developed character. The audience understands little about her academic or economic background, yet, her presence symbolically counters Joaquim's and Blake's experiences within the play. She serves a singular purpose to offer a counterpoint in the representation of Africans by providing a critical voice concerning the continued presence of Europeans in Africa. Her characterization of Neibert and his symbolic interests are reductive, but she is emphasizing the strained relationship that developing countries have with key global interests.

Alongside Ama, Neibert is another figure trapped in the hotel. He is described as "a Belgian tourist and adventurer."[23] His presence adds irony to the serious tone of the play. Ama explains that Neibert "wandered into the mission a week ago," and she presents him as a lost tourist an interloper.[24] However,

Neibert claims that he has been "living amongst the Mbuti in the forest," and because of this experience, he is "no longer Belgian."[25] Neibert's presence in Africa is dubious. He claims to be searching for a mysterious group called the "agogwe," but Ama suggests that Neibert's presence is more nefarious. She argues that Neibert objectifies African culture through his performance: "It is our culture. Our culture. You may admire it, study it, but you can't travel here, put on a robe and take possession of it."[26] Nottage problematizes Neibert's behavior through Ama's admonishment and through his national identity. As a Belgian, Nottage makes a subtle allusion to the catastrophic impact that Leopold II had on generations of Africans living in the Congo.[27] Neibert's presence is an affront to locals like Joaquim who live with the consequences of Belgian policies.

The tension between Mr. Blake and Joaquim impacts every person in the hotel. The action moves quickly when Joaquim takes Mr. Blake's gun at the end of act 1, and a hostage situation is created. Symbolically, Joaquim seizes power but struggles to wield it effectively because he has no true vision for his next steps. Like everyone else in the hotel, he is trapped by the rain, but Joaquim's seizure of Mr. Blake's gun changes the power dynamics within the space. If the Imperial Hotel represents the vestiges of colonialism, then Nottage uses the hostage situation to characterize the problems of decolonization on the stage. What happens when people who have struggled for freedom suddenly gain power? Nottage asserts that they mimic the depictions of power they have seen. In act 2, Joaquim performs authority through his mistreatment of the hostages. One example is when he orders the group to remove their shoes. As the hostages stand at attention, "Joaquim pretends to play target practice with the pile of shoes. He picks through the pile and chooses the best pair."[28] Ironically, the best pair belongs to Mr. Blake. Joaquim enjoys his new shoes and all they represent. He walks confidently in them and presents an air of authority to his captives, but his demonstration is false. Although he has assumed power by taking the gun and shoes from Mr. Blake, he is not a leader. As a former child soldier, Joaquim only knows how to follow orders. Through Joaquim, Nottage posits the difficult road for liberty for decolonized people. Fanon that "during the colonial period the people are called upon to fight against oppression; after national liberation, they are called upon to fight against poverty, illiteracy, and underdevelopment. The struggle, they say, goes on. The people realize that life is an unending contest."[29] The hostage event represents a microcosm of the problems that newly liberated people face through decolonization. Freedom is messy. Joaquim represents countless communities historically dehumanized through colonization struggling to assert their independence. However, the demands of nation building are not easily achieved when your life's work has been dedicated to fighting. How does a soldier flourish in the midst of a tenuous peace?

The final encounter between the two represents an awkward dance between the symbolic colonist and colonized. At the beginning of act 2, Joaquim took Mr. Blake's shoes. By wearing them he asserts a connection, but he can never truly walk the path of Mr. Blake. Nottage symbolizes their differences when Joaquim demands that Mr. Blake kneel before him in an effort to "set things right."[30] Joaquim questions Mr. Blake, asking, "[D]o you know what I'm going to ask you to do?"[31] Mr. Blake guesses that Joaquim wants him to kiss his shoes, so he kneels and kisses Joaquim's feet. Mr. Blake laughs, which enrages Joaquim. As a result of this indignity, Joaquim asserts that "it will never be the same."[32] Nottage does not explain Joaquim's meaning. However, Mr. Blake understands that Joaquim will never submit to him again. Symbolically, the colonized affirms his own humanity by standing up against a symbol of continued power in Africa. In response, Mr. Blake lunges at Joaquim, wrests the gun from his hands, and murders Joaquim. The others signal their dismay over the death, but no one could conceive of a different way to resolve the conflict.

The conclusion of *Mud, River, Stone* is bleak, because the narrative reflects hard truths about decolonization. When imperialists "symbolically" depart their former colonies, they leave lingering issues that the burgeoning nations struggle to solve. These problems often result in a continued reliance on economic and political support from their former captors. Nottage does not provide any meaningful solutions for the real problems symbolically dramatized in the play, yet her work functions as a consciousness-raising activity by presenting a counternarrative to the news clips that gloss over humanitarian crises in postcolonial states.

CHAPTER 4

Reclaiming a Voice from the Past in *Las Meninas*

Lynn Nottage exposes absences within historical narratives in her play *Las Meninas*. In March 2002, *Las Meninas* premiered at the San Jose Repertory. Directed by Michael Donald Edward, the play starred Rachel Zawadi Luttrell and Mercedes Herrero. In an interview with Linda Winer, theater critic for *NewsDay*, Nottage describes the premise of her historical play: "*Las Meninas* is the *true* story of the romance between the Queen of France, the wife of Louis the XIV, the magnificent Sun King, and an African dwarf named Nabo, who was given to her as a gift. I say true because I did extensive research, and I found that this was the case. They had a daughter who was put in a convent where she lived for her entire life."[1]

Nottage's focus on truth in her description of the play reveals her authorial agenda. History is often depicted through a singular lens. We take for granted that the perspectives presented in history are honest, but unvarnished truth often requires multiple perspectives to present a complete impression of an event or person. Nottage excavates the Palace of Versailles for perspectives that help craft a more thorough image of the King, his court, and his political agenda. In this way, Nottage adopts a similar strategy to Alice Walker's decision to fight back. Walker describes this impulse as an attempt to fight for forbearers so that they will "not be lost to us."[2] Nottage continues the recovery tradition that previous African-American female writers began, not by reclaiming a literary foremother but by recognizing a lost Black princess. In *Las Meninas*, Nottage promotes restoration by exhuming Louise Marie-Thérèse and thrusting her into the center of the discussion of the court of Louis the XIV. She forces the audience to review what they have been taught about the past.

Louise Marie-Thérèse, also known as the Black Nun of Moret, is a historical figure who has not been thoroughly examined. Ultimately, the work considers the painting *The Black Nun of Moret* as a historical artifact. What is known of the figure's life and parentage has been lost to history. However, some court documents remain that suggest a deeper connection between the nun and the French royal family. The Black Nun of Moret's story is brought to life to testify to her parentage before she takes the habit and dismisses all worldly concerns. Louise Marie-Thérèse's narrative style challenges the audience to think about the narratives they ingest on a daily basis. How does the framework for understanding these occurrences change when a new perspective is introduced? *Las Meninas* considers that question through Louise Marie-Thérèse's testimonial. Nottage's focus on perspective in the play questions why some historical figures are lauded, and others are forgotten. The truth of Louise's subject position emerges through her tone as she beckons the audience to listen attentively to her origin story: "Shhh! Close the door! Shhh! I'm not demented as the Mother Superior might have you believe, and no you won't go blind if you listen. . . . Now quiet, sweet sisters, and I will tell you again. This is the true story of the seduction of Marie-Thérèse. . . . The Queen of France."[3] Louise's story is told urgently in a secretive manner to the audience for several reasons. The story explores an affair between two dissimilar characters that are drawn together out of a shared isolation in the French court. Queen Marie-Thérèse is a Spanish-born royal married to Louis XIV to alleviate war. In the play, her outsider status is symbolized through her inability to speak the French language effectively. Conversely, Nabo, a native of Dahomey, a kingdom within present-day Benin, is bought and sent as a gift to the Queen from her uncle. Nabo longs to escape Europe and return home. The idea that an enslaved African could connect with a monarch challenges social expectations of the time, which results in the eventual cover-up of this fraught relationship.

Despite their respective positions, monarch and slave manage to create Louise, and her existence is a symbol of defiance that King Louis XIV seeks to erase. Nottage's text enters the expansive space that historians, artists, and dignitaries have left regarding the life and death of Louise Marie-Thérèse. Although Louise Marie-Thérèse was deprived of her royal status, Nottage intercedes in this erasure and creates a space for Louise to tell the story of her birth before she is effectively silenced by committing her life to Christ. In this play, Nottage dramatizes the life of the forgotten princess by filling the stage with her story. To reclaim Louise, the circumstances surrounding her erasure must be addressed. Thus, the relationship between Queen Marie-Thérèse and Nabo is narrated to the audience by their daughter before she takes her vows. Louise describes the circumstances that bring queen and jester into relationship while contemplating her place within the social order.

In *Las Meninas*, Nottage crafts a historical play that questions the truth of historical records by emphasizing the agendas of historians. Louise's voice introduces a new perspective about the history of King Louis XIV's court at Versailles, which highlights how fabrications are interwoven within historical accounts. King Louis XIV's image as the Sun King was crafted and sustained by a state system invested in maintaining his authority. The erasure of Louise was a calculated attempt to ensure that his deified image remained untarnished, but the portrait *The Black Nun of Moret* and excerpts from court memoirs demonstrate that his enterprise was not completely successful. Nottage's play works with and against historical records to shed light on a marginalized figure during this time. As Louise recounts the actions leading to her birth, the audience participates in her historical recovery, though she fears that she "will be lost to history."[4]

Historical Perspectives of Portraits of Royalty

The following is from a production note to *Las Meninas*: "In the library of St. Genevieve in the Latin Quarter of Paris, there is a simple unsigned portrait of an African woman in nun's habit: Louise Marie-Thérèse, the Black Nun of Moret (1664–1732). Cloistered all her life, this African-featured nun took the veil at the late age of thirty-one in 1695."[5] However, biographers of Louis XIV disagree on what exactly happened to the child who was born in 1664. Antonia Fraser suggests, "Marie-Therese would give birth to another daughter Marie-Anne in 1664 who died after six weeks."[6] However, Anthony Levi contends that a child born "in 1664 may have been stillborn."[7] Historians disagree about the circumstances surrounding the birth of Queen Marie-Thérèse's child, but the rumor of a Black baby born to the Queen persists, compounded by the unsigned portrait that bears witness to a noble Black woman born the same year. The woman in the unsigned image looks out at the viewer providing no details about the context surrounding her birth, yet, the portrait attests to her life and survival. With this obscure historical image in hand, Lynn Nottage enters the frame of the portrait and considers the perception of the woman looking out. The once-silent voice of Louise echoes through *Las Meninas*, as multiple perspectives provide dimension to her secret story.

The title of the play takes its name from Spanish artist Diego Velázquez's painting *Las Meninas*. Within that painting, an artist stands aside from his work, looking out at a subject the audience does not fully see. What is most visible to the audience is the foreground of the painting, which includes images of the painter, children, a nurse, two dwarfs, guards, and a mirror reflecting whom the painter is painting: King Philip IV of Spain and his wife, Mariana. The title of the work, *Las Meninas*, translates to "ladies-in-waiting," which refers to the caretakers of the young child in the portrait, Princess Margaret Theresa. Critics have long espoused the visual beauty of the 1656 group portrait, highlighting the various angles and perspectives created within the work. Most famous perhaps is Michel Foucault's rumination, "In the depth that traverses the picture, hollowing it into a fictious recess and projecting it forward in front of itself, it is not possible for the pure felicity of the image to ever present in a full light both the master that is representing and the sovereign who is being represented."[8] For Foucault, the significance of the painting lies in its ability to reveal and obscure while simultaneously preventing the viewer from completely grasping the image the painter is painting and the scene within the painter's studio. This visual paradox within the painting provides Foucault a foundation for his analysis where he emphasizes how the audience's perspective of "the very subject" impacts their perception of said subject.[9]

Later, a modern master reviewed and reinterpreted the subject of *Las Meninas*. In 1957, Pablo Picasso composed fifty-eight images that reinterpreted Velázquez's masterpiece. Most critics view this series as derivative compared with his earlier, more original works. John Berger claims, "Picasso often reconstructs the whole picture. But in terms of content the original painting is even less than a starting point. . . . It remains a technical exercise. If there is any fury or passion implied at all, it is that of the artist condemned with nothing to say."[10] Robert J. Miles further criticizes Picasso, stating that he "produced an image that hinted at the promise but embodied all the problems of re-presenting icons of shared versions of the national imaginary in an unwillingly self-conscious way."[11] Both critics condemn Picasso for reworking a masterpiece without transforming it. However, both misunderstand the importance of reference in the work. Picasso's *Las Meninas* series should be seen as a continuation of Velázquez's earlier work with perspective. By playing with shape, character, and scope, Picasso interacts with the idea of perspective that Velázquez introduces in *Las Meninas*. The conversation surrounding Picasso's series resembles a viewer who is unwilling to interrogate the past. preferring instead a stable view of historical events and images. Instead, Picasso challenges modern viewers of historical images to consider how the artistic lens applied to a subject impacts the audience's impression. Picasso suggests that multiple frames or perspectives simultaneously impact a subject. His invention resides in his ability to destabilize one singular perspective, instead choosing to vary aspects of the scene while not fundamentally changing the overarching subject. He performs a version of what Nottage attempts in her play. In an intense focus on Louise through the space of Versailles, Nottage shifts the frame while holding the royal court fixed in position. This allows the viewer the opportunity to reexamine the image and to focus in on areas that she highlights through Louise's interactions with the court.

Las Meninas is a fitting title for Nottage's play, as Louise is a lady-in-waiting to begin a new life in the cloister at Moret. During this pivotal moment in Louise's life, Nottage encourages the audience to actively observe the circumstances surrounding Louise's birth and her erasure from history. In act 1, scene 1, the stage directions indicate that the royal couple "sit for a portrait, which is painted by an expressionless man. Members of the court adoringly watch their King and Queen."[12] Nottage frames this narrative through the lens of watching eyes. The key players within the royal family are watched, and their behaviors are dissected by onlookers, which lays the groundwork for court gossip. Members of the play's audience watch the choices the actors make, given who is viewing their performance. In this way, Nottage creates a space for the audience to evaluate the court's key players when they remove or apply performative masks for the benefit of courtiers present.

During the time of the play, artists created works that deified their patrons. Thelma R. Stockho asserts that French leaders, including Louis XIV, supported artists to ensure "irrefutable proof of their importance."[13] This pattern of commissioning artists to create works that emphasized the glory of the monarchy was politically motivated. They used art as propagandistic tools to assert their right to rule by connecting their images to success and the glory of the state However, Nottage unpacks these images through the conflict that is present within the painting of the royal couple. The King seems dismissive of the whole process, despite the political function of the piece, while the Queen makes a clumsy attempt at conversation with her husband. Neither character is focused on the task at hand, which reveals the competing agendas that both characters display in the scene. The King behaves in an aloof manner as the court gazes upon him. Meanwhile, the Queen seeks to grab her husband's attention through a conversation about a present she received from her cousin. As this comic scene plays out, the painter is left with the responsibility of crafting a formidable image that portrays both figures nobly, despite their clear incompatibility.

During this intricate performance, Nottage cuts the tension within the scene with the introduction of Nabo. The present that the Queen's cousin has sent is an African dwarf. His appearance in the court shifts the focus from the painting to this new spectacle. Having gained the King's attention, the Queen hopes to induce a performance from Nabo, but he resists stating:

> Nabo: What can one perform after being in a box for three days? I was promised six goats and some beads, and I closed my eyes and I had crossed the ocean. And now I'm scented, powdered and stuffed in a box. If I perform, it's functions of the body, and that Your Majesty is private. Each place I go, they expect me to perform. What? I do not know. And they pack me back in a box and send me on. I've traveled halfway across the world in this box. And I'm tired, tired, tired . . . of it.[14]

This frank response shocks the court and grasps the King's attention, but Nabo refuses to sing or dance for the crowd. Defeating their expectations, the King ultimately departs, leaving the Queen with a new fool to entertain.

Nabo's honesty cuts through the tension present between the distant spouses and provides an opportunity for the Queen to connect with someone else. Because she feels isolated at Versailles, Nabo's distraction provides her with some purpose. Initially she seeks to command Nabo into performing for her. When that fails, she instead takes the opportunity to describe the context of the court to Nabo, an outsider with no allies at court. Gesturing toward the King, the Queen muses to Nabo, "That is your king not nearly as impressive as his portrait."[15] Again, Nottage emphasizes that images do not provide a complete picture of a person. Although countless portraits of Louis XIV exist to promote his status, they do not reveal his shortcomings as a husband or ruler. This backhanded comment informs Nabo of the tensions within the royal family. The center of the narrative does not revolve around the King. The Queen takes center stage, complaining about her unhappiness in France.

The Queen's behavior is indicative of a subject aware of an audience. She is objectified in the court as courtiers orbit her position, but the source of power within her sphere of influence attends to his own needs, while his network of sycophants bolster his deified image. With the King at the center of influence, the painter focuses on presenting him in a good light. However, he does not use his artistic ability in the same way for the Queen.

> Queen: That's not me! You've given me a healthier, more masculine look dan I appreciate. Thin me out, more color in the cheeks, and extend my chin. How come Louis gets color and I don't?
>
> Painter: Your Majesty, I paint what I see.
>
> Queen: No, you paint what I see. . . .[16]

Despite her position of power, the King's image is most important to the realm. As such, the painter frames the King in a sympathetic light. The aesthetic choices he makes do not reflect reality, but they do impart an image that many believe is true. The Queen's encounter with the painter establishes that by showing her in an unflattering light, he tarnishes the image of the King, because her image affirms his power. For the Queen, the reality of her shape and color must be masked, and her perception of self should be reinforced within the painting. In this encounter between the Queen and the painter, Nottage questions how the viewer's perception of a subject alters the character of the subject. If the subject of the image is aware of the viewer's gaze, how can the subject impact the viewer's perspective? Nottage destabilizes the view of the image of the King and Queen as infallible historical figures to create a context that allows for Louise's position within this world. The focus on appearances and reputation foreshadows later choices made to alter historical records by omitting Louise's life from history.

Politics of a Forbidden Encounter

Royal marriages in the seventeenth century had little to do with romance. Instead, the unions were a tool to ensure power remained within the grasp of a small affluent group. As such, marriages were used as a strategy to broker political deals and ensure peace. Queen Marie-Thérèse from Spain was a part of such a union. The Franco-Spanish War (1639–1659) ended in part because of the Peace of the Pyrenees treaty, signed in March 1659. Henry Kamen articulates that the agreement included "a key clause to the treaty arranged for the marriage of Maria Theresa, daughter of Phillip IV, to Louis XIV of France."[17] The Queen's transition to French customs was a difficult one. At Versailles, the Queen did not meet the French standards of beauty, which contributed to her outsider status. Antonia Fraser notes that the Queen tended toward "plumpness"; additionally, her fashions exaggerated her hips and prevented people from coming close to her.[18] Although educated, she lacked an affection for literature and the arts, which her husband adored. In short, according to Kamen, "with her jewels, her false hair, and her touch-me-not skirts . . . she was neither graceful or alluring."[19] Nottage plays up the Queen's incompatibility with her husband to establish her alienation in court. Dramatizing her loneliness, the Queen's behavior becomes more erratic as she lashes out at her husband and demands that he spend time with her. The resulting standoff affirms the King's mistress La Vallière's status as favorite and leaves the Queen licking her wounds. To her aid comes an unlikely source: Nabo.

Nabo consistently encourages the Queen during outbursts. "That's right, Your Majesty, don't let him take your pride. Once he has that, you're bankrupt."[20] The nature of Nabo's relationship with the Queen changes dramatically after her fight with Louis. The Queen loses her composure and reveals her loneliness to Nabo. This rare demonstration of vulnerability on the Queen's part results in an embrace.

> Queen: What kind of Queen am I that quivers in the arms of a fool?
> Nabo: What kind of fool am I that cradles in my arms a queen? Shall I let you go, Your majesty?
> Queen: Only if you like?
> Nabo: Pardon me if I say that I like very much holding Your Majesty.
> Queen: And I like very much being held.[21]

Nottage romanticizes the encounter between the Queen and Nabo, which complicates the nature of their relationship. As the Queen's fool, Nabo is obliged to obey his mistress, yet the interactions in this scene suggest a tenderness that contrasts the political barriers that separate them. The overarching image of both characters is one of desperation. Nabo is a man who is eager to return home after a long trek abroad. His time in Europe has been fraught with repetitive exchanges between various houses. In this moment, Nottage humanizes Nabo through his desire to hold and be held. He is a man who craves a connection. His isolation in Europe differs from the Queen's in that he does not possess the privilege that she takes for granted. Although she is a political pawn, she still possesses a level of power that is foreign to Nabo. The Queen has an obligation to the King and her nation to bear offspring to continue the lineage for the crown. Having a sexual encounter outside of her marriage puts her at great risk for punishment. The consequences for Nabo are dire. By consummating a relationship with the Queen, he has effectively signed his death sentence. His choice to continue is an interesting one. Whether he is motivated by lust or sees this act as the ultimate protest for his condition within the court, the risk he takes in this moment characterizes an individual on the precipice of disaster. Despite the certainty of consequences for their sexual encounter, both proceed.

Their escapade is narrated by Louise. Her impression of the tryst between her mother and father is framed from a daughter's perspective: "With a kiss he now possessed the Kingly prize. With a kiss he tasted empires past and future. With one tender kiss she drew him and they faced the possibility of freedom.[22] Louise's impression of her parents is one of defiance. For her, this singular moment reveals a thoughtful act in which two dissimilar figures rebel against the social institutions of the French monarchy. How might this perspective influence her opinion of herself? Instead of seeing herself as illegitimate, through this lens, Louise understands that her life is a symbol of agency. By giving

Louise a voice at the moment of her conception, Nottage provides her with the opportunity to respond to the criticism that follows her mother and ends the life of her father shortly after her birth. The relationship that her parents cultivated provides them with a moment of harmony, despite the fraught spaces each occupies within the court. The nature of their relationship is imperfect and tinged with danger, yet the messiness within their coupling provides Louise with a nuanced view of their encounter.

La Vallière, the Mistress Who Reveals the Truth

The reputation of Louis XIV reinforces the idea that he was a much-desired lover. Despite his marriage, he maintained several extramarital relationships with mistresses throughout his life. Two of these mistresses' memoirs document their relationships with the King and the rumored birth of a Black child to the Queen. Madame la Marquise de Montespan and the Duchess Louise de La Vallière both were central figures at Versailles during the time of the scandal. The King's affections were fickle and shifted constantly. Nevertheless, these women featured prominently in the King's life at the Court of Versailles from 1661 to 1677. Their proximity to power afforded them the opportunity to be privy to court intrigue. Their respective memoirs both reference that the Queen gave birth in 1664, and they both include the race of the baby. Madame de Montespan's is the clearest account of the scandal maintained in written records. In her memoir, she claims:

> I have already told how the envoys of the King of Arda, an African prince, gave to the Queen a nice little blackamoor, as a toy and pet. . . . The Queen was delivered of a fine little girl, black as ink from head to foot. They did not tell her this at once, fearing a catastrophe, but persuaded her to go to sleep, saying that the child had been taken away to be christened. . . . The little African was sent away, as may well be imagined. . . .[23]

Nottage includes La Vallière within her play seemingly combining aspects of both mistresses into the character. Additionally, Nottage includes a note at the beginning of the play that incorporates elements of Madame de Montespan's memoir. Nottage's use of historical artifacts to frame Louise's narrative shows that, despite the erasure of Louise from royal records, people were aware of the origins of the nun's birth.

Throughout the play, Nottage shows La Vallière as a rival for the King's affection. Because of the intimate nature of her relationship with the King, she is consistently seen in conflict with the Queen. For example, at the end of the royal portrait sitting, the Queen questions the King.

Queen: Where are you going?
King: Pardon me, I have pressing affairs of state to attend to.
(The King takes La Vallière's hand. The entire court stirs.)[24]

The King's behavior before the court lacks compassion for the Queen. This moment sets the groundwork for the eventual connection between Nabo and the Queen, as she longs to be comforted. Moreover, the scene highlights that the whims of the King impact who is seen as a favorite within the court. Toward the beginning of the play, La Vallière is a clear favorite and holds a position of esteem through her relationship with the monarch, but his favor is not guaranteed as the King has multiple mistresses whom he waffles between, leaving La Vallière at the mercy of his whims.

Throughout the play, Louise stands on the margins, serving as a plot device that connects disparate characters who establish the historical context surrounding her birth. Within this context, Louise consistently speaks directly to the audience about the story she narrates as the audience observes the action. This stylistic choice reminds the audience of the purpose of the narrative as the characters interact. Nottage additionally allows Louise to interact with various characters throughout the play. These interactions take place in her cell at the convent where various members of the court visit her. Nottage's dramatic decision does not reflect the historical reality of the experience of the Black Nun of Moret. However, the narrative choice affords Louise an opportunity to comment on her status at the convent. The conversations that she has with the Queen and La Vallière provide her a space to vent about her circumstance, which reveals her unwillingness to become a nun. The most powerful example of Louise voicing her disinterest in a future at the convent occurs with La Vallière, who initiates the conversation by providing a context for her visit: "The Queen asked me to come in her stead. A fever took hold three days ago and it rages through her body. . . . I know how much she looks forward to visiting the convent. She always seems reinvigorated after conversations with you. I've come to try my hand. I too need to be uplifted."[25] This initial introduction confirms that most of the women attached to the King are unhappy. The Queen bemoans her husband's inability to remain faithful. A perspective La Vallière understands now that she is "no longer in fashion."[26]

Although other members of the court have visited Louise in the play, none have been forthcoming about her origin.

La Vallière: Don't you know? Hasn't anyone told you?
Louise: Told me what?
La Vallière: This is going to cheer me up.

Louise: What are you saying?

La Vallière: The Queen is your mother, Louise. You are never going to leave here.[27]

It is a curious choice to allow La Vallière the responsibility of informing Louise of her heritage. No historical record exists that provides context for this meeting or any such meeting with the Queen. The historical space provides Nottage with an opportunity to imagine Louise's perception regarding her imprisonment at the convent. The dramatic scene results in a violent outburst in which Louise cuts herself and laments "Royal blood? What use is this blood if it makes a prisoner of me?"[28] Louise's response conjures the pain of the historical figure's experience by emphasizing her separation from family and the realization of her future: a life spent in forced solitude. Louise's realization of her status as an illegitimate child of the Queen establishes the context for her conflict with the King and ultimate erasure from history.

Conclusion

The unsigned portrait of the Black Nun of Moret is a visual artifact surrounded by questions. Was the nun the daughter of the Queen of France or some other key figure in French society? Conflicting historical documents deny or confirm her parentage. Regardless of the conflict, her image remains and provides a space for discussion. Black figures have been consistently brushed to the margins of historical texts from before the seventeenth century to the contemporary period. Nottage crafts a nuanced play that dramatizes what happens when a silenced voice speaks back. Nottage examines the role of perspective within art through Louise's narration and uses this lost voice as an opportunity to suggest that historical perspectives require multiple accounts to understand the complexity of an event or person. *Las Meninas* is an attempt to put the pieces together and uncover the narratives surrounding the life of this obscure figure. If figures like Louise can be buried, they likewise can be exhumed. The painting is the evidence of her existence, but to truly exhume her body from the edges of history, the full range of images presented as demonstrative of the French monarchy's power must be reevaluated as well. Nottage attempts this feat in her play by questioning the circumstances of Louise's birth and her dismissal from history. *Las Meninas* questions the authenticity of singular narratives pertaining to historical events by allowing perspectives that challenge the dominant narrative to be heard. In this way, Nottage reclaims Louise from the shadows and affords her perspective a spotlight.

CHAPTER 5

Marriage and Respectability in *Intimate Apparel* and *Fabulation*

In an interview with the *New York Times*, Lynn Nottage describes her 2004 play, *Fabulation*, as "a modern-day companion piece to *Intimate Apparel*" because both works feature women battling "existential self-crises."[1] Originally commissioned and produced by South Coast Repertory in Costa Mesa California, *Intimate Apparel* was directed by Kate Whoriskey and opened in Baltimore, Maryland, on April 18, 2003. It later opened in New York City at the Roundabout Theatre Company in April 2004. Directed by Daniel Sullivan, the New York production starred Viola Davis, Lynda Gravatt, Arija Bareikis, Corey Stoll, Lauren Velez, and Russell Hornsby. *Fabulation, or The Re-Education of Undine* premiered at Playwrights Horizons in New York City in June 2004. Also directed by Kate Whoriskey, the cast included Charlayne Woodard, Melle Powers, Stephen Kunken, Robert Montano, Saidah Arrika Ekulona, Keith Randolph Smith, Daniel Breaker, and Myra Lucretia Taylor. Lynn Nottage and director Kate Whoriskey have a longstanding collaboration that began with the play *Intimate Apparel*. Their collaboration continues with her most recent works.[2]

Set in 1905, *Intimate Apparel* follows the story of a southern migrant in New York City, Esther Mills, who has a sewing business selling lingerie to wealthy women on Fifth Avenue as well as women who work in gentleman's clubs. Esther's business offers her a bit of autonomy but more important, it situates her within the private spaces of women across town where she is privy to their dreams and aspirations. Her prowess as a seamstress, along with her ability to remain discrete about the conversations that she hears in private, affords her an opportunity to create fruitful relationships. Over the course of her eighteen years in New York City, she manages to save money toward her true ambition: opening a beauty salon for African-American women. Her entrepreneurial goal drives her throughout the play, as she works tirelessly to earn the money for her enterprise. Ultimately, Esther's dreams are thwarted when she marries a Barbadian immigrant named George Armstrong. She gives him her money as a way to show her commitment, but this choice backfires when he abandons her.

In *Fabulation*, set in the present, Undine Barnes Calles undergoes an epic fall from grace as an established public relations manager organizing events for wealthy Black business owners. To achieve her high-powered role, on graduation from college she disowned her family and given name, Sharona Watkins. To climb the social ladder, she crafts a new bourgeois identity to promote her success. Once her husband, Hervé, steals her money and leaves her penniless and pregnant, she returns home to deal with the reality of single motherhood and an identity that she left behind years ago.

On the surface, these characters have very little in common. Esther is not ashamed of where she comes from. In fact, she develops a craft that affords her opportunities throughout the city that would position her to maintain an independent life beyond marriage, but this is not the life she chooses. On the other hand, Undine is a character who makes calculated choices from her time in college throughout her professional career, but she chooses poorly when marrying. Both women are ambitious individuals who are striving to be successful. What success means for each woman is connected to the historical context of the times in which they live. In their own way, each woman is striving to uphold an image of Black womanhood that outlines their success. For Esther, success means involvement within the community and participation in social clubs where married women are the primary members. For Undine, success means distance from anything remotely identified with the stereotypical images of the ghetto or a welfare queen. Undine wants to "have it all," which includes a man who, she assumes, is socially mobile and affluent. She wants to fulfill the image of the modern woman who has both a relationship and a career. Ultimately, both women are unable to carve out a unique space where they can establish their own sense of success, because they are too concerned with the norms of success within their communities. Nottage qualifies their falls from grace as existential crises, but a better way to understand the connection between Esther and Undine is through their inability to understand their value independent from men. The identities of both women are so closely aligned with the status afforded to them through their marriages that when these relationships fail, the women are left struggling as they attempt to rebuild their lives.

Mrs. Dickson and the Realities of Marriage in *Intimate Apparel*

Esther's story is framed by her work and her despair. The scenes of *Intimate Apparel* are outlined by a garment connected to the story. Act 1, scene 1, is titled "Wedding Corset: White Satin with Pink Roses." The audience views Esther busy at work. The stage directions describe her as "a rather plain thirty-five-year-old African American woman. . . . She is all focus and determination."[3] Esther lives in a boarding house owned by Mrs. Dickson. In the scene, Mrs. Dickson is throwing a wedding party for Corrina Mae, a young woman who recently wed. Instead of joining in the festivities, Esther focuses on completing a wedding present for the new bride. Her commitment to the wedding corset provides her with a reasonable excuse to miss most of the party. This introductory scene explores Esther's jealousy and her unwillingness to participate in the celebration. Esther turned thirty-five recently, and no one remembered. Esther does not slight Mrs. Dickson for forgetting her birthday, because she understands that Corrina Mae's wedding was at the forefront of her mind. However, the slight is another reminder that weddings are one of the most important social events for women. At thirty-five, Esther is beyond the marrying age customary for young women in the boarding house. As such, she begins to believe that her desire to marry will be unfulfilled, because thus far no likely suitors have attempted to court her. Esther has lived with Mrs. Dickson for eighteen years and has witnessed twenty-two other young women get married and move away. The constant succession of women moving in and out further reminds Esther of her single status. Ultimately, Esther fears that she will never marry. This fear informs her actions in the play.

Years before, Esther journeyed from the South and found a home with Mrs. Dickson, but she dreams of having a home all her own. Esther's sadness envelopes the text as she accepts that she will never have the opportunity to wed. "I should be happy for them, I know, but each time I think, Why aint it me?"[4] One reason for Esther's single status is the ratio of eligible Black men in New York in comparison with eligible Black women. Jacqueline Jones outlines that Black "women who left home along the southeastern seaboard helped to create unbalanced sex ratios in Philadelphia (116 black females to 100 males in 1900) and New York (124 to 100). In 1905 one-quarter of all adult black women in New York lived alone or in a boarding house."[5] As African-American women migrated north for more economic opportunities, their marital options were impacted by the availability of men. Esther fears becoming an old maid, because the community in which she dwells seems to have no space for unmarried women.

Within the play, Esther demonstrates a desire to fulfill the standards of womanhood of her time. Defined by nineteenth- and early twentieth-century standards, womanhood was connected to domesticity and idealized through the roles women played within familial structures. Women standing outside of this structure were not valued within society. Known today as the "cult of true womanhood" or the "cult of domesticity," Black and White women were valued on the basis of their ability to fulfill specific feminine standards. As defined by Barbara Welter, "the attributes of True Womanhood, by which a woman judged herself and was judged by her husband, her neighbors and society could be divided into four cardinal virtues—piety, purity, submissiveness and domesticity. Put them all together and they spelled mother, daughter, sister, wife—woman. Without them, no matter whether there was fame, achievement or wealth, all was ashes. With them she was promised happiness and power."[6] These principles evolved in the twentieth and twenty-first centuries into what is commonly known as "respectability politics." Mikki Kendall defines respectability politics as "an attempt by marginalized groups to internally police members so that they fall in line with the dominant culture's norms."[7] Kendall rejects the idea of respectability politics when she claims that "No woman has to be respectable to be valuable."[8] Esther desires to marry because she thinks that her status as wife would increase her value within her community. She would be able to navigate spaces where older Black single women are not welcome. In her mind, her single status undermines her value in society.

For Esther, the only thing worse than being an old maid is making a bad choice in marriage. Mrs. Dickson encourages Esther to participate in Corrina Mae's wedding festivities to find a possible suitor. Specifically, she encourages Esther to flirt with a man named Mr. Charles, but Esther is wary of the proposition.

> Esther: But he's been coming to these parties for near two years and if he ain't met a woman, I'd bet it ain't a woman he after. I've been warned about men in refined suits. But still, Esther would be lucky for his attention, that's what you thinking. Well, I ain't giving up so easy.
>
> Mrs. Dickson: Good for you. But there are many a cautionary tale bred of overconfidence. When I met the late Mr. Dickson he was near sixty and I forgave his infatuation with opiates, for he come with this rooming house and look how many good years it's given me. Sure I cussed that damn pipe, and I cussed him for making me a widow, but sometimes we get to a point where we can't be so particular.[9]

Esther rebuffs Mrs. Dickson's suggestions regarding Mr. Charles. She believes that he might not be heterosexual and, although she is past her prime marrying and childbearing years, she refuses to give up her hope of finding a more suitable match. However, Mrs. Dickson's revelations regarding her own marriage initiate a discussion about the sacrifices that wives make. Her husband was an older man and an addict. On the surface, these attributes are not ideal. Nevertheless, her monogamous relationship has bestowed her with some benefits. As a widow, Mrs. Dickson has fulfilled societal expectations of marriage, but she occupies the privileged position of no longer being beholden to her husband's desires. The business that he left her affords her economic independence. Her situation is unusual in that she is single and independent, but she does not bear the negative connotations of singledom as an old maid. From her vantage point, her marriage was a positive economic enterprise, although her relationship was not ideal.

Mrs. Dickson's personal experience challenges Esther's idealized image of her future husband by dramatizing the sacrifices required of a wife. In New York, there are few eligible bachelors who pique Esther's interest. However, she receives letters from a man named George Armstrong. He is a Barbadian immigrant working "in Panama alongside Carson Wynn, your deacon's son."[10] Their initially harmless exchanges develop into a more serious affair when George proposes marriage. Mrs. Dickson cautions Esther to consider the possibilities available to her before plunging ahead into the unknown with a man whom she has never laid eyes on. Mrs. Dickson cautions Esther, warning "You know, you don't have to do this."[11] However, Esther fears that if she does not marry, her life will not have value. "I'll turn to dust one day, get swept up and released in the garden without notice."[12]

From Esther's perspective, a woman must marry to have value. She perceives the opportunity to wed George Armstrong as a final chance at happiness. Esther's romantic image of love and marriage encourages Mrs. Dickson to reveal a part of her personal story to dissuade Esther from expecting too much from marriage, a story in which she was encouraged to marry to avoid the shame of being single. Mrs. Dickson reveals, "you see, my mother wanted me to marry up. She was a washerwoman, and my father was the very-married minister of our mission."[13] The shame that Mrs. Dickson's mother felt because of her relationship with a married man impacted the lessons she taught her daughter. The lessons imparted values regarding love, and as a single woman, her mother worked hard as a washerwoman to provide for her child. She encouraged her daughter to "marry good" so she could avoid "the markings of labor."[14] The values that Mrs. Dickson learned reveal how women were devalued during her time. As an institution, marriage affords women with the opportunity for status within a patriarchal society that values compulsory heterosexual relationships. Mrs. Dickson confesses that she married because she was "thirty-seven years old, I had no profession and there wasn't a decent colored fella in New York City that would have me."[15] Mrs. Dickson posits that Esther has an opportunity that most women do not have: She has a profession. Esther's work makes her valuable and necessary despite her marital status. Esther disagrees. She lacks the personal experience of romantic relationships to weigh against the privilege of independence. She also operates within a community that regards wives as superior to old maids. Although having a husband is a desirable status for an older single woman within her cultural context, Mrs. Dickson's experience offers an opportunity for reflection. What does it mean to be a wife? What benefits are there for married women? Do these benefits outweigh the opportunity to live as a single woman of independent means?

Two Choices

In Frances E. W. Harper's (1859) short story "The Two Offers," Harper chronicles the story of two African-American cousins.[16] One woman has two offers of marriage. The other has none and is perceived as an old maid. The first woman chooses a man who comes from a good background and has presented himself well during their courtship, but ultimately he ends up being a poor choice, as he cheats on her, drinks heavily, and abandons her. Harper's story cautions women about the choices they make in marriage. Esther's plight resembles some elements of Harper's work. Throughout *Intimate Apparel*, Esther is presented as a woman with limited options. In New York, she has not found an African-American suitor who meets her standards for a spouse. The lack of options within her community leads her to make a hasty decision and marry George Armstrong.

The reality of George does not resemble the images that Esther fell in love with during her courtship. Nottage juxtaposes the outside image of romance with the reality of the Armstrongs's relationship. At the end of act 1, Nottage creates a tableau on stage symbolizing their wedding. "A projected title card appears above their heads: 'Unidentified Negro Couple, ca. 1905.'"[17] The title card symbolically explains the true nature of their marriage. The couple does not know one another well enough to have entered a committed relationship. However, Esther fell in love with George's charisma in his letters and agrees to their union when he proposes in his final letter. After they are married, the reality of his brusque personality sours their interactions. On the first night they share together, Esther presents George with a beautiful smoking jacket, which he "tosses on the bed."[18] George is not pleased with the efforts that Esther makes to welcome him to the city. Instead, he wants to engage physically with her immediately, but Esther resists:

> Esther: Couldn't we wait a bit?
> George: Minister say, "man and wife."
> Esther: Please, I'd like to know about your mother or your birthplace, Bar-ba-dos. Something I don't know. That wasn't in the letters. Something for us, right now.[19]

This initial encounter dramatizes their different values. George is not the romantic man from his letters. He demands the privileges of marriage without fulfilling his marital obligations as a husband.

Additionally, George's motivations for moving to New York are not clearly articulated. During an argument, he claims "'e drink in words of this woman. She tell 'e about the pretty avenues, she tell 'e plentiful. She fill up 'e head so it have no taste for goat milk, she offer me the city stroke by stroke. She tantalize me with Yankee words. But 'e find not she."[20] George blames Esther for the difficulties he experiences in New York. He aspires to build things, but he finds that, as a Black man, there are few opportunities for the types of jobs that would utilize the skills he cultivated in Panama. There are domestic jobs available, but these do not fulfill his desires. The racism that George experiences in New York leaves him discouraged and angry. He turns this anger on his wife by refusing her romantic advances and cavorting in taverns, which leaves Esther alone at home. Esther and George are disheartened by the reality of their circumstances within their marriage. Esther has longed for a companion who would elevate her status, so she can attend church socials that single women are not invited to attend. George dreamed of New York as a place of great opportunity where he could establish a foundation building skyscrapers in the growing metropolis. However, the reality of the city and the lack of shared values within their marriage foreshadows their eventual separation.

Before George abandons Esther, he reveals that he did not write the letters during their courtship. He confesses that he paid "an old mulatto man. I paid him ten cents for each letter, ten cents extra for fancy writing."[21] Similarly, Esther concedes that she did not write her letters either. However, she claims that the information within her letters accurately described her personality and intentions. In act 1, Esther longed to be married. She envied her housemates who found partners, despite the evidence of the reality of marriage for women like Mrs. Dickson. Esther did not think that, as a single woman, she could amass the same value as a married woman because she juxtaposed the images of old maid and wife. She believed that if she were married, her value would improve, but her experience with George established the opposite. Ironically, George reaffirms Mrs. Dickson's earlier claims. Esther's desperation to marry results in her making a poor choice. She loses her savings, but she gains a valuable lesson. Esther learns through her relationship with George that her value as a person is not dependent on her marriage with a man. Her newfound knowledge does not change the values within her community, but her failed marriage provides her with a sense of self-worth.

Mr. Marks stands in opposition to George Armstrong, although they share many similarities. Like George, Mr. Marks is an immigrant. He is a Romanian Jew who comes from a long line of tailors. He has established himself as a textile merchant selling fabric and accessories to seamstresses and tailors alike. His hardworking background establishes Mr. Marks as another character born outside of New York who has migrated to the big city for economic opportunities. Although, Mr. Marks is a White man, he maintains a subtle flirtation with Esther before she marries. Mr. Marks is a better fit for Esther than George Armstrong. They are connected through the garment business. As a textile salesman, Mr. Marks has an appreciation for the crafts that Esther creates. He explains, "my father sew, my brother sew, yes, for the finest families. But I don't have the discipline. . . ."[22] Because tailoring runs in his family, he connects with Esther through her work. Mr. Marks consistently saves special products for Esther, because she is one of his favorite customers. She is a favorite because of her attention to detail, not because she spends the most on his products. As a result, he saves items for her that he thinks she will like. For example, when buying stock for his store, he notices a silk: "I see it and think Esther Mills will like."[23] His observation, although subtle, suggests his affinity for Esther. He understands her tastes and makes choices when buying goods that will appeal to her. Their affection never extends beyond their pleasant encounters. Once, Esther grabs Mr. Marks's hand and he flinches. This saddens Esther, because she believes that his response indicates a racist attitude, but he explains:

> Marks: No, no. I'm sorry. It's not that. Please. My religious belief doesn't permit me to touch a woman who isn't my wife or my relative.
>
> Esther: Oh, I see.
>
> Marks: It is the rabbinical law, not mine.[24]

Much like Esther, Mr. Marks clings to his cultural values. However, he assures her that the values that create boundaries between them are not his laws, although he adheres to them. Nottage dramatizes the tensions between cultural standards and individual desires in the relationship between Esther and

Mr. Marks. As a Black Christian woman, Esther believes that she must marry a Black Christian man to fulfill social expectations, despite her feelings for Mr. Marks. Similarly, Mr. Marks upholds religious customs that were passed down. He is adamant that he is not a racist. He does not want Esther to misunderstand his attitude toward her. Nevertheless, the dynamics of race and religion prevent Esther from establishing a loving relationship with Mr. Marks.

After marrying George, Esther visits Mr. Marks twice. During the initial encounter, she has an emotional outburst and promises to never return, stating, "please, I think you know why."[25] The unspoken attraction she feels for Mr. Marks reveals itself after she marries George. Esther is unhappy in her marriage because George lacks integrity. He does not respect his wife's work or appreciate her as an individual. Esther's experiences with Mr. Marks contrast her encounters with her husband. The sadness she feels reveals her awareness that the match she has made is not a good one. After act 2, scene 5, it is clear that George has left her. Esther pays a visit to Mr. Marks. In this encounter, the audience witnesses a changed woman. Esther has transformed because of her experience with George. She now understands her value as an individual, with or without a male partner. She gives Mr. Marks the smoking jacket she made for her husband from the silk that Mr. Marks had saved for her, a gift that Mr. Marks accepts after protest. As he tries it on, she remarks that "it fits wonderfully."[26] The smoking jacket is a symbolic token for the husband Esther does not have. The imperial silk that Mr. Marks saved for Esther has been connected to four characters in the play. Initially, Esther gives it as a gift to George, who gives it to Mayme, a prostitute for whom Esther often creates lingerie. After Esther retrieves the jacket, she gives it to a man who is worthy of such a gift. Mr. Marks is compatible with Esther in many ways. He is a respectful man who values his religious customs and beliefs. He treats Esther with genuine kindness and admires her prowess as a seamstress. There exists a genuine affection between the two characters in every scene they inhabit. However, an interfaith and interracial marriage is impossible in 1905. The tragedy of Esther's situation is that she cannot consummate her relationship with Mr. Marks, given the social expectations of the time.

A Fall from Grace in *Fabulation*

Fabulation, or The Re-Education of Undine, focuses on a fall from grace by a powerful public relations agent, Undine Barnes Calles. The title alludes to fables or stories that impart lessons. Unlike *Intimate Apparel*'s Esther, Undine begins her narrative at the top of society and undergoes a dramatic plummet after the news that her husband has disappeared with all her money. What follows is a dark comedy that considers the choices people make as they climb the ladder of success. Sandra G. Shannon describes *Fabulation* as "a social satire and 'comeuppance tale' about a comfortable middle-class African-American woman's discovery, ironically during the course of bouts with poverty, despair and an unexpected pregnancy."[27] Lessons abound for Undine, as she must reconcile her current situation with stigmas, both real and imagined, that she has battled her entire life.

For Undine, success came with a carefully traveled path that has minimized her connection to her familial community. However, the descent she experiences sends her back to her roots in Brooklyn to rediscover who she was before the hype and glamour she took for granted in her carefully crafted façade. Shannon's description of Undine's narrative as a "comeuppance tale" underscores the sense of her punishment throughout the play. How have Undine's actions led her to this moment of catastrophe? Nottage uses Undine's tragic story to impart a warning to others desperate to escape similar situations. Success should not disconnect a person from their community. Without a strong identity grounded in cultural values, success is fleeting. Undine learns this lesson after her fairytale life begins to unravel. Her success story is doomed to fail, because it is constructed from lies. In act 1, Undine describes her assent to success:

> I went to Dartmouth College, met and mingled with people in a constructive way, built a list of friends that would prove valuable years down the line. And my family . . . they tragically perished in a fire—at least that's what was reported in *Black Enterprise*. It was a misprint, I nevertheless embraced it as the truth. Fourteen years ago I opened my own very fierce boutique PR firm, catering to the vanity and confusion of the African American nouveau riche. And all seemed complete when I met my husband Hervé at a much too fabulous New Year's Eve party at a client's penthouse. Eleven months later we married. Two years later he had a green card. Why? He permitted me to travel in circles I'd only read about in Vanity Fair.[28]

From her time in school, Undine's life has focused on appearances. Her lower-class family living in the Walt Whitman housing projects did not connect with the image she crafted for her future. To fit in the highest echelon of society, she constructs a new identity that erases the legacy of poverty from her history. Without her family to reflect her true origins, she can fashion a new identity. Once known as Sharona Watkins, she adopts the name Undine Barnes, the first name she learns from Edith Wharton's the *Custom of the Country* "in an American Literature course at Dartmouth College."[29] Her new name is a step away from her home and an entry into a world built on deception. Her identity is crafted with care, but her choice in spouse lacks the same attention to detail.

On the surface, Hervé plays the part of an Argentinian playboy, and like Undine, he's all performance with little substance. Undine realizes his deception too late, and her understanding signals the beginning of Undine's downfall as she grapples with the fragments of her carefully constructed life. Nottage characterizes Undine's reckoning with direct addresses in which Undine develops a rapport with the audience. This strategy affords Undine an opportunity to reveal her true feelings despite her ongoing performances with the characters she engages. Thus, with the audience, she takes on a confessional tone in which she processes her undoing as she moves toward an emotional awakening.

Navigating Social Institutions

Nottage signals Undine's reckoning with a physical and emotional breakdown that Undine names "Edna." Ironically, Edna is also the name of Kate Chopin's protagonist from her 1899 novel, *The Awakening*, where a woman similarly undergoes an awakening when she begins to question her purpose as a mother and wife.[30] In *Fabulation*, Edna is described as "a pain in my chest so severe that I've given it a short, simple, ugly name. . . ."[31] The physical pain Undine feels is an effective plot device that shifts Undine from her corporate office to a local clinic where she encounters Dr. Khdair.

> Dr. Khdair: I believe you've suffered a severe anxiety attack. It's not uncommon.
>
> Undine: Anxiety? Me? On no, I don't think so.
>
> Dr. Khdair: And why not?
>
> Undine: Anxiety happens to weepy people on television news magazines.
>
> Dr. Khdair: Well, all of our tests came back normal. But there's one other thing Ms. Calles. I ran some routine tests and, congratulations, you're pregnant.[32]

The discussion between Undine and her doctor reveals Undine's misconceptions concerning Blackness and mental health. Her dismissive tone regarding anxiety suggests an inability to reconcile the tension that she currently feels as a result of the tumultuous changes in her life. Mikki Kendall argues that "the myths of the Strong Black Woman . . . influence the perception that women who are not White do not experience a full range of emotions, much less suffer from the same mental health issues."[33] The collapse of Undine's marriage and career have brought on stress and panic. After learning of her husband's theft, Undine's fears surface. "Bankruptcy—no. That implies that somehow I failed."[34] The carefully constructed character that Sharona has created over the past fourteen years reflects the impact of internalized anti-Blackness. She has performed as a "strong Black woman" throughout her professional career, but this performance is false. By changing her name and distancing herself from her family, Sharona has concocted a superhuman character who does not need support. In her mind, she is a self-made woman who can weather the storms of life on her own. According to Melissa Harris-Perry, the strong Black woman archetype represents an "idealized description" of Black women that challenges stereotypes of Black femininity by countering with descriptions of Black women as "unassailable, tough, and independent."[35] The strong Black woman archetype, embodied in Undine, undermines Sharona's humanity. She can be strong and sensitive, but the role she plays does not allow for balance.

Undine's pregnancy represents an opportunity for growth. Throughout the play, Undine is unable to accept the reality of her circumstances. Her fall in class creates new problems that she must grapple with. One such problem is the bureaucracy of the medical industry. Without insurance, Undine lacks the means to afford effective prenatal care. Nottage dramatizes Undine's bureaucratic tango at the Department of Social Services. As a public relations representative, Undine took pride in her ability to get things done, but she struggles to get any help from her local governmental offices because of seemingly simple bureaucratic procedures. At the office, Undine undergoes a humiliating encounter with a caseworker who is more concerned with order than with helping people. After waiting in a line for two hours, she is informed that she needs to fill out a form, which she does begrudgingly. Later, after standing in line again, she realizes that she filled out the wrong form and would have to try again. The frustration that Undine experiences is played for comic effect in the scene, but through the humor, Nottage exposes the difficulties that poor people face in trying to access aid. The system that Undine navigates is created to wear people down and prevent them from moving forward, but she is too stubborn to allow that outcome.

After finally receiving welfare benefits, she meets with a doctor who questions why she has waited so long to seek medical treatment. Undine's response is a blistering takedown of America's health care system. "Listen, I tried to make an appointment with my regular doctor, but she wouldn't see me without health insurance. I attempted to make an appointment with another gynecologist, but it seems I needed a referral from the local clinic. I went to the local clinic, but I didn't have the appropriate paperwork. Apparently when I became poor I was no longer worthy of good health care."[36] Undine's diatribe is interrupted as the doctor instructs her to schedule her next appointment, but Undine wants an abortion. She has not planned to have a child, and she currently does not have the means to provide for herself or the child. However, the doctor informs her that she is about six and half months pregnant, far beyond the period when an abortion would be possible. The reality of the impending birth frightens Undine.

The image of the life she carefully constructed lies about her in tatters. Now she is faced with the possibility of being a welfare queen. Patricia Hill Collins defines the welfare queen as "a highly materialistic, domineering, and manless working-class Black woman. Relying on the public dole, Black welfare queens are content to take the hard-earned money of tax-paying Americans and remain married to the state."[37] This racial stereotype reflects a patriarchal and heteronormative construct that argues that Black women do not maintain healthy marriages and thus create abnormal familial structures. Hill Collins suggests that the Black welfare queen stems from a need to create a controlling image to dissuade women from "demanding equity in access to state services."[38] Undine does not fulfill this stereotype, but she is treated as a negligent mother by her caseworker and doctor, who lecture her about following rules. Nottage uses Undine's misfortune to show the audience the problems within two separate social institutions within the United States. The Department of Social Services and her gynecologist represent two disparate systems meant to help women when they are facing hard times, yet both representatives fail to see the humanity in Undine and view her as a number or worse, a statistic. The irony is that Sharona has made choices throughout her life to avoid this type of treatment, but with just a few missteps, her calculated life has fallen apart.

A Critical Look in the Mirror

Esther Mills and Sharona Watkins are women who grapple with pervasive images that falsely define Black womanhood. Their inability to fully escape these stereotypical representations emphasizes the limitations they face. Harris-Perry states "when they confront race and gender stereotypes, black women are standing in a crooked room, and they have to figure out which way is up. Bombarded with warped images of their humanity, some black women tilt and bend themselves to fit the distortion."[39] Harris-Perry describes the difficulties that Black women face in existing authentically. Their lives are framed by what Frances Beal describes as "double jeopardy," where Black women experience a tenuous space in the United States that is due to the double oppression of racialized sexism.[40] Esther and Sharona are aware of the images that define Black womanhood and attempt to occupy roles within their respective landscapes that afford them some individual privilege. Despite the different historical eras they occupy, both are unable to escape these demeaning images, because they spend most of their time reacting to them. This reactionary posture undermines their ability to envision an autonomous place in society, which results in both women living unfulfilled lives.

CHAPTER 6

Sexual Trauma and Survival in *Ruined*

Ruined was commissioned by the Goodman Theatre in Chicago as a part of its 2007 New Stages Series and premiered in November 2008; it later opened at the Manhattan Theatre Club in February 2009.[1] Matthew Blank observes that the play asks several key questions: "Set in a small mining town in Democratic Republic of Congo, this powerful play follows Mama Nadi, a shrewd businesswoman in a land torn apart by civil war. But is she protecting or profiting by the women she shelters? How far will she go to survive? Can a price be placed on a human life?"[2] The play was directed by Kate Whoriskey and features Saidah Arrika Ekulona, Quincy Tyler Bernstine, Cherise Boothe, Chris Chalk, William Jackson Harper, Chiké Johnson, Russell Gebert Jones, Kevin Mambo, Tom Mardirosian, Ron McBee and Condola Rashad.

The road to the stage commenced several years before, as Nottage undertook multiple journeys to Africa to source material for her work. Originally, Nottage intended to draft a version of Bertolt Brecht's *Mother Courage and Her Children*, but she changed course after a series of visits to various African countries. With the help of a Guggenheim Fellowship, starting in the summer of 2005, Nottage ventured to Uganda to research for a play she intended to write about war and women. "I traveled to the region because I wanted to paint a three-dimensional portrait of the women caught in the middle of armed conflicts; I wanted to understand who they were, beyond their status as victims."[3] Nottage's travels abroad provided her with a wealth of information from survivors of the atrocities of the genocide in the Democratic Republic of Congo (DRC), Uganda's neighbor. Her interactions, primarily with women who survived wartime sexual violence, painted a very different picture from the one that she read about in the news. The Center for Preventive Action reports that "since 1996, conflict in eastern DRC has led to approximately six million deaths. The First Congo War (1996–1997), began in the wake of the 1994 Rwandan Genocide, during which ethnic Hutu extremists killed an estimated one million minority ethnic Tutsis and non-extremist Hutus in Rwanda (DRC's neighbor to the east)."[4] The continuous instability in the region resulted in a fractured state where rival factions fought for control. Nottage used her experience in Uganda to craft a dynamic portrait of the cost of war. In *Ruined*, Nottage analyzes the trauma of war from the perspective of a group of women in the Congo. Nottage does not explore the causes of war but, instead, examines the results of the conflict on vulnerable people like women and children and asks key questions about survival. What does survival cost survivors?

War and Rape in the DRC

The war in the DRC that Nottage examines in *Ruined* has its start in the mid-1990s. Central to this war is the rape and sexual assault of women, men, and children. Nottage focuses specifically on the impact of rape during war on women and the consequences for their communities. Sarah Brownmiller, an American journalist and feminist activist, defines rape through choice: "If a woman chooses not to have intercourse with a specific man and the man chooses to proceed against her will, that is the criminal act of rape."[5] Key to Brownmiller's definition is the concept of consent. Throughout *Ruined*, women rarely can claim agency over their bodies and lives. As a result, their bodies are used as political objects for men to demonstrate their political power. The specific circumstances of the war in the DRC provides countless opportunities for men to harm women who are vulnerable to callous political actors. Sara Meger, scholar of international relations and political sciences, contextualizes the war, explaining that "Ugandan and Rwandan-backed rebel groups in the eastern provinces of Congo attempted to overthrow the government in Kinshasa, armed conflict has been waged consistently between a shifting configuration of rebel groups and the Congolese army in an apparent attempt by each group to secure access to vast deposits of valuable minerals throughout the region."[6] In war, sexual violence is a tool used to control the civilian population during the conflict. Rebel groups as well as Congolese-backed forces used sexual assault through rape, gang rape, and sodomy to inflict terror on women, children, and men. The goal of these specific violent acts was to demonstrate power over Congolese communities and to ensure the cooperation of local townspeople. However, Meger also argues that war creates opportunities for armed forces to commit sexual abuse because of their sexual appetites. Conflict creates a chaotic space that "disrupts the normal morals and rules of society."[7] Incidents of rape increase as traditional moral expectations are diminished through the lack of law and order. Thus, the lack of oversight or retribution provides soldiers with an opportunity to brutalize defenseless populations while they simultaneously pursue a political end through battle. In *Ruined*, Nottage emphasizes two political forces at play in the region. One force is associated with the rebels and rebel leader Jerome Kisembe. The Congolese side is headed by Commander Osembenga. Both figures struggle to control their soldiers' baser instincts throughout the play, which emphasizes the chaos on both sides of the fray that contributes to the brutalization of women's bodies.

The women in *Ruined* represent a composite of the individuals Nottage interviewed during her travel abroad. Although she refrains from incorporating their narratives verbatim, she does include elements of the violence they faced. The title of the play alludes to a specific form of sexual violence that many women faced during the war in the DRC. The sexual violence explored in the play is twofold. First, there is gang rape perpetuated by soldiers on both sides of the war. One character, Salima, is raped in front of her baby and abducted. She is transported to the soldiers' camp, where she faces frequent assaults and is forced to work for the camp by cooking and cleaning for them. International relations and conflict scholar Miranda Alison explains that when soldiers perform a group sexual assault, the act "cements a sense of loyalty between men and those who might not rape individually do rape collectively in a group assertion of masculinity."[8] In essence, their behavior establishes a comradery through a collective ability to assault women. The second form of rape identified in the play is connected to mutilation. In this form, women are sodomized with tools including sticks, guns, and bayonets. This form of rape is disconnected from the perpetrators' sexual pleasure and rather presents a hypermasculine attack on the femininized body. Women who face this specific form of wartime sexual violence, if they survive, suffer from incontinence and vaginal fistulas. In both cases, women face physical, emotional, and social repercussions for the harm experienced. The women whom Nottage features all physically survive their experiences of rape but are fundamentally changed because of their traumatic experiences. While dealing with the emotional toll that their assaults cause, Nottage's characters face ostracism from their communities.

Ruined is set in a tavern/brothel in a community within the DRC. The bar is run by Mama Nadi. She is a character that walks a fine line throughout the play. She desires to maintain a business and provide for herself while not choosing a clear side in the war. Ben Brantley notes, "The play in which Mama Nadi appears is not unlike the house over which she presides. 'Ruined' [. . .] is a comfortable, old-fashioned drama about an uncomfortable of-the-moment subject. But whereas Mama, a latter-day variation on Brecht's *Mother Courage* (the Brecht play that partly inspired 'Ruined'), uses hominess and familiarity to shut out the terrors of war in Congo, 'Ruined' craftily creates the same atmosphere to bring those same terrors to our attention."[9] Neutrality proves hard to achieve, as she services both rebels and nationalists. At Mama Nadi's bar, all patrons are welcome if they have the money to pay for alcohol or companionship. Her ambivalence toward the sides in the dispute emphasizes their similarities. Both groups demonstrate boorish behavior toward women, but if they refrain from fighting in her bar, she permits them to stay. Challenges arise in the play when the soldiers act violently toward patrons or her workers. Mama must diffuse tense situations or run the risk of losing her business.

As a businesswoman, Mama claims to take care of her girls, but she also uses them to establish economic independence. Throughout the play, the audience witnesses three of Mama's girls: Josephine, Salima, and Sophie. Josephine, the daughter of a chief, was raped and cast out of her village. She dreams of leaving Mama Nadi's place with a frequent client who promises to situate her in a comfortable apartment in the city. Salima is a wife and mother who often reminisces about her life before she was abducted and gang raped by rebels. Sophie is a beautiful former student who was "ruined" when she was raped with a bayonet by soldiers. The physical assault has destroyed her reproductive system, which prevents her from sexual work at the brothel. However, she uses her reading and mathematics skills to help Mama Nadi conduct business. Additionally, she performs as a singer for weary travelers, miners, and soldiers who frequent the bar. Josephine, Salima, and Sophie have been cast out of their respective communities because of the sexual violence they experienced. Global health journalist Stephanie Nolen explains that "there is such stigma associated with rape in Congo—where female virginity is prized and the husband of a rape survivor is considered shamed—that rape survivors are routinely shunned by husbands, parents and communities."[10] Thus, the brutality that the women endure marks them as undesirables, and the community that they called home will provide no sanctuary. The lack of choices makes them vulnerable. Although Mama Nadi provides her workers with food and shelter, the price for their sanctuary is costly.

Masculine Power in *Ruined*

The patrons of Mama Nadi's bar provide a landscape to understand masculine power in the play. Even male characters who do not participate in the war display privilege associated with their sex. The significance of their male privilege is best seen through their mobility. Whereas the women in Mama Nadi's bar seem fixed in place due to the war and the sexual abuse they have experienced, men are permitted to move about more easily. Many men frequent the bar, including soldiers and nearby miners, but the characters Christian and Mr. Harari move most freely. Christian is described as a traveling salesman in his early forties. He provides a valuable service for Mama Nadi as he smuggles in products necessary for her clientele, including cigarettes. His ability to travel across the country and secure goods provides him with access to information. This access assists his work and provides a meaningful exchange when he interacts with Mama Nadi. Initially, Christian's flirtatious demeanor suggests a true affection with Mama, but sometimes he uses his affections to garner favors. In addition to exchanging products, he also functions as a human trafficker. In act 1, scene 1, Christian barters with Mama Nadi over the sale of two women: Salima and Sophie.

> Mama: Did you at least tell them this time?
> Christian: Yes. They know and they came willingly.
> Mama: And . . .?
> Christian: Salima is from a tiny village. No place really. She was captured by rebel soldiers, *Mayi-mayi*, the poor thing spent nearly five months in the bush as their concubine.
> Mama: And what of her people?
> Christian: She says her husband is a farmer. And from what I understand. Her village won't have her back. Because. . . . But she's a simple girl, she doesn't have much learning, I wouldn't worry about her.
> Mama: And the other?
> Christian: Sophie. Sophie is . . .
> Mama: Is what?
> Christian: . . . is . . . ruined.[11]

Initially, Christian presents himself as a charismatic businessman, but his transaction with Mama Nadi displays a disturbing part of his trade. Nottage hesitates to condemn Mama or Christian for their actions, because they are aiding women in desperate need of shelter. With few options, an opportunity to work at Mama Nadi's is a last chance for relative safety. Ultimately, Christian reveals that Sophie is his niece, so his actions are an attempt to find her a haven because her family has refused her, but the only option he can secure for her is at a bar/brothel. This puts Sophie in a dangerous position where she will have to continuously interact with unstable men. Furthermore, Christian's conversation with Mama suggests that some of the women he has trafficked have not been informed of the requirements for their employment. Women who have already been brutalized through war face a new shock when they are compelled to service soldiers or struggle to find food and safety on their own. Through Christian, Nottage depicts the callousness of war—yet he does not escape unscathed. In the beginning of act 1, Christian refuses alcohol at the bar and will only drink Fanta sodas. As the war wages on, he begins to drink whiskey and beer to calm his nerves regarding the escalating danger. Christian devolves into alcoholism as he is unable to absolve himself from the corrupt role he plays in the conflict.

Similarly, Mr. Harari demonstrates male privilege through his ability to navigate between the capital city and backwater locales for business. Mr. Harari frequents Mama Nadi's bar and is described as a Lebanese diamond merchant. His job provides much needed context regarding the ongoing political instability in the DRC. Throughout the play, miners or soldiers try to barter with Mama Nadi for drinks or other items with unrefined coltan. Despite the politically fraught space, Mr. Harari maintains operations within the country. His presence speaks to the country's rich mineral and gem deposits. These natural resources make the DRC a pivotal location for mining, because modern technology is dependent on some of these resources for manufacturing and technological innovation. Nottage explains:

> We're beneficiaries of the abundance of resources that exists there. About 90 percent of coltan, the semi-conductive mineral that's used to fuel cell phones and laptops, comes from the Congo. We're invested in the instability there. As long as they can extract coltan cheaply, we continue to buy our cell phones and laptops for very little. I want Americans to acknowledge that we have a stake in the war that's being fought there."[12]

Nottage's commentary reverberates through Mr. Harari's character. His presence suggests the wealth that resides within the DRC, and he is willing to take risks to recoup financial rewards.

While frequenting Mama Nadi's bar, Mr. Harari drinks and patronizes the sex workers. Specifically, he develops a relationship with Josephine as a favorite client, but he is a salesman at heart. He sells her a dream that she wholeheartedly believes in. Josephine states, "Mr. Harari is going to take me. Watch out, Cherie, he's promised to set me up in a high-rise apartment. Don't hate, all of this fineness belongs in the city."[13] Mr. Harari manipulates Josephine and plants ideas of escape into her head. He gives her presents and promises to whisk her away from the drudgery she endures, but he has no intention of helping Josephine. He uses her body as her other clients do. The dream that he sells Josephine is a cruel tactic used to garner favor with her. Although it provides her with momentary hope, she will ultimately learn that his intentions were not honorable. Mr. Harari plays a role in the DRC. He buys and sells stones. His role extends to the services of women, too. Mr. Harari shows the audience how men with a bit of status can operate within chaotic regions. They prey on the desperate wishes of poor men and women with no real intention of helping them climb out of the holes of poverty in which they are stuck. On the surface, Mr. Harari seems harmless, but the emotional toll he levies on the women in the play is damaging.

Women's Ruined Reputations

Men shape the political landscape of the DRC in *Ruined*, and women reflect the consequences of their power. The physical assaults that civilian women face in the play impact their reputations and connections to their communities. Katherine Albutt, et al., explain that "stigmatisation, rejection, and abandonment are prominent features of survivors' experiences of sexual violence in eastern DRC."[14] When women most need community support, many are shunned. The ongoing trauma that Josephine, Salima, Sophie, and Mama Nadi navigate in the play reflects the ongoing ramifications of wartime sexual violence. The play examines how women's bodies are targeted in war. The shifting allegiances between warring factions in the play emphasizes the similar strategies that soldiers use to wage war. In *Ruined*, women's bodies are the terrain where men battle. Their intermittent skirmishes leave few people whole. Instead, the characters dramatize the lingering impact of war. The women are left to try to survive after they have been victimized, with little opportunity for justice. Their survival relies on their ability to adapt to the ever-changing political landscapes they inhabit. The fate of each woman remains dependent on her ability to divert the violent attention of men who exert their will with few penalties. The sexual violence experienced in this play transforms characters physically and mentally. Those who survive the physical attacks are haunted by their past lives. Their new degraded state emphasizes the chasm between their current status and their experience before the assault. Survival in *Ruined* requires women to learn how to acquiesce to men's desires while maintaining some sense of safety. Some characters are better performers than others. The cost of survival proves too high for some, as they cannot reconcile their current condition.

Josephine

At Mama Nadi's bar, Josephine's primary role is as a sex worker. The assault she suffers before her employment leaves her with physical and emotional scars she struggles to hide throughout the play. In act 1, scene 3, Nottage describes the physical evidence of Josephine's torture: "Josephine takes off her shirt, revealing an enormous disfiguring black scar circumventing her stomach. She tries to hide it."[15] However, Josephine has little privacy, because she shares a room with Salima and Sophie. As she tries to cover her physical disfigurement, she lashes out at both women. Her adversarial relationship with her fellow sex workers evidences her misplaced anger. Josephine projects her insecurities onto women occupying a similar position because, like her, they are vulnerable. Instead of creating a communal sanctuary through their shared experience, Josephine lashes out at them because her trauma reflects a distrust of women: "What are you looking at?"[16] When she feels vulnerable, she becomes defensive. This survival strategy stems from past betrayals in her community.

Before she was sexually assaulted, she was a chief's daughter. Her current job conflicts with her past status as a respected member of her tribe. She explains: "My father was chief! The most important man in my village, and when the soldiers raided us, who was kind to me? Huh? Not his second wife: "There! She is the chief's daughter!" Or the cowards who pretended not to know me. And did any of them bring a blanket to cover me, did anyone move to help me? NO!"[17] She blames her community for her lost position and assault. She reasons that the second wife's betrayal encouraged the rapist soldiers' attack. During the siege of her community, the second wife made a desperate plea to protect herself and sacrifice Josephine. Her status was seen as an opportunity to inflict cruelty on her father. Consequently, Josephine's bitterness toward her community exposes the fragility of a woman's status in her tribe. Her power stemmed from her connection to a powerful man, and once that man loses power, her legitimacy is questioned as well. Josephine learns negative lessons from this experience. She continues to value relationships with powerful men, as evidenced through her aspirations with Mr. Harari, but she also becomes distrustful of women. In her experience, when marginalized women are vulnerable, one strategy for survival is to attack other similarly vulnerable women to ensure safety. Josephine's experience translates as cruel insults to her fellow sex workers. Her haughty nature connects to her past privileged position that she lost because of the war and the sexual abuse she suffered. In her current role, she is required to teach newcomers the expectations of working at Mama Nadi's. However, her relationship with the women at the bar is tainted from her past sexual assault. Although her status once afforded her an honored place within her community, her position was previously used against her. As a result, she continues to grapple with the emotional and physical scars of her community's betrayal.

Josephine's trauma connects to her desire for escape. This ambition is shown through her relationship with Mr. Harari. His constant attention affirms her sense of self. In turn, Josephine focuses on her outward appearance as a catalyst to change her circumstance. She clings to the possibility that her attractiveness will provide her with an avenue of escape. Her focus on women's beauty products, as evidenced through her collection of fingernail polish and fashion magazines, suggests that she connects the possibility of escape with attractiveness. Mr. Harari capitalizes on Josephine's desperation by admiring her beauty. Although he pays for the time he shares with her, he also gives her false hope by suggesting an escape.

> Mr. Harari: Such loveliness. Doesn't she look beautiful?
> Mama: Yes, very. *Karibu.*
> Mr. Harari: I just might have to take you home with me.
> Josephine: (*Excited*): Promise.
> Mr. Harari: Of course.[18]

Mr. Harari's empty promises are a tool he uses to seduce Josephine, but she's complicit in his deceit through her uncompromising belief in his sincerity. Her job at Mama Nadi involves constant cruelty as the men pay to have sex with her. She is not empowered through her physical exchanges with these men. She does not choose those with whom she has encounters, nor does she keep any of the money she earns from her work. Her position is a hopeless one, and Mr. Harari preys on her vulnerability to ensure her compliance. Despite the reality of her circumstances, Josephine holds onto Harari's false promises as a symbol of possibility. The hope she has for a future escape provides her with momentary peace to survive the degradation she experiences at Mama Nadi's bar.

Salima

Salima is a character who has lost all hope. Unlike Josephine, Salima's memories of the past fuel her sadness in the present. She reminisces about her past as a mother to baby Beatrice and a wife to husband Fortune. The relationship she had with Fortune was forever changed by her abduction and rape. She describes the horrors of her experience to Sophie. "Do you know what I was doing on that morning? I was working in our garden, picking the last of the sweet tomatoes. I put Beatrice down in the shade of a frangipani tree, because my back was giving me trouble. . . . Where was Fortune? He was in town fetching a new iron pot. . . . One of the soldiers held me down with his foot. He was so heavy, thick like an ox. . . . His foot was so heavy, and it was all I could see as the others . . . 'took'" me.[19] The impression of the brutal gang rape and abduction lingers with Salima. She lost her family on that morning. Her baby was murdered by the soldiers, and she was rejected by her husband and family on her return. The war destroyed her family and her home. As Sharon Friedman clarifies, in war, like in *Ruined*, some of these women are doubly victimized: sexually assaulted and impregnated or left unable to reproduce; furthermore, they must endure shaming by male members of their families and communities, who perceive the violation of "their" women as another form of defeat."[20] Salima experiences a double victimization through the rape and expulsion from her community. Working at Mama Nadi's extends her trauma through continued sexual exploitation. Mama Nadi's patrons treat the women with cruelty and continue to use their bodies for sex. Her work puts her at risk of sexually transmitted disease and pregnancy. Either would end her time at Mama Nadi's and result in an uncertain future.

Throughout the play, Salima struggles with memories of home. The past represents pleasant and unpleasant experiences. Salima blames Fortune for her hardship. She explains that after returning from her five months of captivity, Fortune, "the man that I loved since I was fourteen, chased me away with a green switch. He beat my ankles raw. . . . He was too proud to bear my shame . . . but not proud enough to protect me from it."[21] Although Salima valued her time as a mother and wife, she understands that her grievances prevent her from achieving a reconciliation. Salima's experience at Mama Nadi's is complicated by an unwanted pregnancy and Fortune's reemergence. She becomes pregnant from her sex work and fears termination from her job. Although she does not enjoy her work at Mama Nadi's, there are few options for her if she leaves. Moreover, Salima does not trust Fortune's motives, because his past behavior privileged his reputation over his obligations to his wife. Salima is a tragic figure in *Ruined* because she has no opportunity for survival. After her body is violated, she serves one purpose for the men of her community. There are no safe spaces to provide her sanctuary. Her experience teaches her that marriage is not a safe space for women. Even if her husband took her back, there would be the issue of the baby conceived at the brothel. Toward the end of the play, her realization of the limited opportunities inspires her to commit suicide. She proudly announces, "You will not fight your battles on my body anymore."[22] Salima's worth was connected to her relationship with men. She fulfills her obligation to her family by marrying and bearing a child, but her inability to fend off the soldiers diminishes her worth in their eyes. When Fortune later searches for his wife, it is too late for Salima's redemption. Although some might view her actions as a protest, the character's death does little to change the circumstances of her loss of community as a result of the sexual exploitation she suffers.

Sophie

Of the three sex workers featured in *Ruined*, Sophie is the most defiant. Christian explains that before Sophie was "ruined," she was a student. As such, her academic background affords her different opportunities in the bar. Unlike

Josephine and Salima, Sophie is not subjected to continual sex work. The assault she experienced results in a vaginal fistula, which makes continued sex work an unlikely option. Instead, she helps Mama Nadi manage the books and sings for the patrons. Her access to money and the patrons grants her the chance to escape from Mama. She hides money and covertly plans to leave with Salima, boldly stating, "we won't be here forever."[23] Notably, Sophie's ambitions are not connected to men. Unlike her peers, her sense of self is established through her intellect. She does not envision returning home or leaving with a man; instead, she desires a surgery to reconstruct her damaged reproductive and digestive systems. Ultimately, her attempts to escape are thwarted when Mama discovers the stolen money. Nevertheless, Sophie establishes through her cunning an indominable spirit and her desire to direct her own course.

Throughout the play, the sex workers must manage the expectations of the male customers. Sophie is in a precarious position because, as a beautiful woman, she is desirable, but her injuries make sex a harmful proposition. Contemporary drama and disability studies scholar Ann M. Fox claims that "being 'ruined' refers to the supposed loss of honor, but, through Sophie's impaired body, it also points to the injuries that some women experience that have been rendered culturally invisible."[24] Fox's point connects to the dehumanization Sophie suffers through her experiences with the men at the bar. The men's aggressive behavior constantly puts Sophie at risk. As they sexually harass her, she lives with the constant threat of rape. One encounter with Commander Osembenga prompts a defiant response from her. Typically, Mama Nadi dissuades the men from engaging with Sophie by distracting them with drink or the services of another sex worker. However, Osembenga's position allows him to make demands that few can deny.

> Osembenga: Come here you pretty pretty thing. What? You don't like what I'm wearing? You don't like men in uniforms? You don't like men, maybe. Is that it?
>
> Mama: Sophie, come here. Let—
>
> Osembenga: Hey. We are talking. We are talking, yeah? Am I ugly? Is that what you're trying to tell me.
>
> Sophie: Let go of me!
>
> Mama: Sophie, shush! Enough. Commander, ignore her, there are other girls for you. Come. Come.
>
> Osembegna: Bring this girl around back, my men will teach her a lesson. She needs proper schooling.[25]

Typically, Mama Nadi effectively dissuades men from interacting with Sophie because she is ruined. However, in this scene, she is unable to distract the

Commander. Nevertheless, Sophie defends herself by rejecting his advances and spitting on his shoes. The threat of being gang raped again pushes Sophie to challenge the Commander. While men dominate the bar with their bawdy behavior, Sophie's rebellion is a final gesture that signals her humanity, despite her continued sexual objectification.

Ultimately, Sophie's defiance does not shield her from sexual violence. In Mama Nadi's bar, Mama's desires supersede the will of her workers. Mama Nadi wants to continue to make money in her bar, so she sacrifices Sophie to the Commander to save her business. She does not defend Sophie; instead, she ensures that the Commander is sexually satisfied by Sophie, which effectively punishes her for rejecting his advances. Toward the end of the play, the war continues to escalate. Although Sophie is allowed to stay in the bar, her future remains uncertain. Without the economic independence necessary to navigate the DRC, Sophie's future prospects seem bleak.

Mama Nadi

The center of *Ruined* is Mama Nadi and her bar. Throughout the war, she shrewdly navigates political tensions by fulfilling men's desires. She presents herself as both savior and taskmaster. This double role results in sudden shifts in her demeanor that testify to her hard-won position. The problem with Mama is that she demands more than she gives. She at once provides a space for ruined women to live but pressures women to prostitute themselves to the same kinds of men who tainted their reputations initially. Throughout the play, Mama walks a fine line, refusing to take sides in the fight that surrounds her. Instead, she chooses her business as a priority and supports whomever has the coin to purchase her wares. However, her bravado is shattered when Sophie challenges Commander Osembenga and jeopardizes her operation. After dissuading the Commander from violence, she demands that Sophie submit to his sexual advances. This choice is a shocking decision, but Mama defiantly defends her perspective. "You men kill me. You come in here, drink your beer, take your pleasure, and then wanna judge the way I run my 'business.' The front door swings both ways. I don't force anyone's hand. My girls Emilene, Mazima, Josephine, ask them, they'd rather be here, than back out there in their villages where they are taken without regard."[26] Mama's monologue neglects the reality of her girls' circumstance. They have nowhere else to turn. She refuses to acknowledge that she is taking advantage of their vulnerable state. Mama's choice to subject Sophie to the depravity of Osembenga underscores her desperation.

Her behavior throughout the play has demonstrated an unwillingness to acknowledge the significance of the political climate surrounding her bar. She chooses to focus on her bar and the services she provides. For Mama, the bar is her refuge and provides the only protection she trusts. Jill Dolan comments, "Nottage modulates the play's tension level, intercutting visits from rebels and government soldiers with more familial scenes of Mama and her girls, trying to establish some sense of a normal life in between the anxious moments with the men, whose brutality and arrogance are interchangeable. Mama and the girls suffer their presence because it puts food in their mouths, but the acts required of them in exchange fray their souls."[27] While the men orbit her bar, the bar symbolically provides her with security. However, Sophie's confrontation with Osembenga emphasizes the unpredictability of their collective circumstances. Mama falsely believes that she is in control, but the men waging war repeatedly remind her of women's powerlessness in this society.

Mama's belief in her power is connected to her insurance policy. In act 1, Mama shows Mr. Harari an unrefined diamond. She keeps it in a special lock box with her money and important documents. This stone represents another option for Mama. If the business does not work out, she can sell the diamond and move away. However, as the conflict nears her bar, she hesitates. Nottage makes two distinctive choices toward the end of the play that undercut the realism she embeds in Mama's character. First, Mama gives Mr. Harari the diamond as payment for Sophie's operation.[28] Second, she succumbs to Christian's advances and seemingly agrees to begin a relationship with him after suddenly revealing that she herself is ruined.[29] Neither choice realistically connects with Mama's character. Consistently, Mama has put her needs before her girls, yet when given the opportunity to escape with Mr. Harari, she offers Sophie a chance for survival. In her haste, she leaves the stone with Mr. Harari, who flees the skirmish, leaving Sophie and Mama at the bar. An escape is never truly possible for these women. However, Nottage concludes the play with Mama embracing Christian. Dolan suggests that this shift transforms the play into "a heterosexual romance, in which Mama and her girls are redeemed by the love of a good man."[30] In spite of this decision, there is no true redemption for Mama or her girls. The play's conclusion emphasizes that women in this community are reliant on the whims of men, which leaves them perpetually vulnerable. Although Mama claims she is an independent figure, her stability is contingent upon serving men.

Conclusion

Ruined earned Lynn Nottage her first Pulitzer Prize for Drama in 2009. However, some were unsettled that the play won this award. Alexis Soloski claims "While the play takes an unsentimental view of the violence afflicting the Congo, it also supplies a love story featuring a startlingly happy ending. The

Pulitzer board noted this emotional appeal, characterizing the play as an 'affirmation of life and hope amid hopelessness.'"[31] The tension some critics felt over this perceived conflict negates the complexity of the play and the complexity of war. War negatively impacts all aspects of life in the play; the relationship between Mama Nadi and Christian provides a glimmer of humanity within the chaos of war. Survival in this play is difficult to manage for single women. Perhaps this relationship is a clever attempt to demonstrate agency over her trajectory.

Wartime sexual violence is not unique to the conflict in the DRC. Historically, wartime rape has been used as a tool to systematically destroy communities since women are viewed as the symbolic vessel of life. Consequently, the violence that women face during war emphasizes their perceived power or powerlessness in society. The men in *Ruined* psychically and physically wage war by violating the autonomy of women. Through rape and mutilation, men demonstrate their power within the chaotic tensions of war. By focusing on the impact of this specific wartime violence, Nottage implores her audience to consider the effect of gender inequality on vulnerable populations. Although this conflict might feel worlds away to theatregoers in the United States, Nottage grounds the global implications on the devaluation of women's bodies through the commodification of minerals and natural resources used in products that most of her audience members have in their pockets. It is this link that emphasizes our collective responsibility to acknowledge our connection, their plight.

CHAPTER 7

Humanizing Performers in *By the Way, Meet Vera Stark*

On December 17, 2004, Lynn Nottage sat for an interview with Linda Winer, a drama critic from *Newsday*, for an episode of her series *Women in Theatre*. During this episode, the two discussed Nottage's upbringing and commitment to crafting multicultural plays that consider identity. Their conversation concluded with a discussion of how Nottage envisions her own identity.

> Winer: There is a lovely quote from you that says, "How I identify myself changes depending on where I am in the room." Could you explain that a little more?
>
> Nottage: Well, you know when you are in a room full of men, I am a woman. When I am in a room full of White women, I am an African-American woman. You know, so it sort of shifts according to the context and how loudly I have to declare who I am.[1]

A part of Nottage's response illuminates the idea that an individual's identity is not static; instead, how people present themselves, especially for minorities, often depends on the contextual realities of an interaction. Where she is and who she is can be articulated differently depending on the cultural context.

Years later, Nottage explores the idea of shifting identities in her 2011 play *By the Way, Meet Vera Stark*. Jo Bonney directed the 2011 off-Broadway run, which starred Sanaa Lathan as Vera Stark opposite Stephanie J. Block as Gloria Mitchell. Ben Brantley observed that "[t]his play has a wonderfully juicy premise. It imagines the back story of one of those talented actresses seen on '30s movie screens almost exclusively in the roles of maids, slaves, or mammies. (Ms. Nottage has said that she was specifically inspired by Theresa

Harris's appearance in the 1933 Barbara Stanwyck vehicle *Baby Face*, but Hattie McDaniel, Louise Beavers, and Fredi Washington come to mind as well.)"[2] In this play, Nottage presents the story of Vera Stark, an African-American actress living in Hollywood working as a domestic for "White" film star Gloria Mitchell. Vera lives with her roommates Lottie and Anna Mae. Vera and her roommates face barriers to their collective goal of starring in Hollywood films because few movies during that time provide African-American actresses with speaking roles or roles that allow them to portray nonstereotypical characters. However, when an intriguing new script for *The Belle of New Orleans*—rumored to contain speaking lines for actresses portraying Black female slaves—comes on the scene, the women find ways to audition for the subservient roles by performing caricatures of Blackness for the director and studio head.

The second act shifts to 2003 during a symposium that considers Vera Stark's landmark performance in *The Belle of New Orleans* and her last interview on the fictional talk show *The Brad Donovan Show* in 1973. Three panelists—a professor, a journalist, and a filmmaker—consider the significance of Stark's performance while contemplating her eventual disappearance from American media. The question that resounds through the second act is "What happened to Vera Stark?" Her whereabouts lead to a robust discussion of her performance of gendered Blackness in film and during her last known interview. As the panel argues over the significance of the performance and Stark's professional career, the conversation shifts to a heated debate regarding the depiction of Blackness on screen. Ultimately, Nottage uses the symposium as a mechanism to investigate the connection between past and present perceptions of Blackness. Nottage exposes the tenuous nature of racial performance by scripting comedic consciously stereotypical performances in act 1 and reflecting on the subversive and problematic tensions within these representations of race in act 2.

Nottage examines racial performance by emphasizing how an audience shapes the choices performers make. In act 1, Vera, Gloria, Lottie, and Anna Mae craft racialized performances of Blackness and Whiteness shaped by the presence of a White male gaze. The women present exaggerated racialized performances that reflect the director's and producer's biases back to them. The actresses understand the men's expectations of them and choose to perform stereotypically to be cast in *The Belle of New Orleans*. Although the women do not challenge the men's narrow impressions of race, their performance encourages viewers of the play to consider the complexity of racial identity through their enactment of stereotypes. Next, Nottage complicates her critical examination of racial performance in act 2 through the symposium. In this act, Nottage contrasts the director's and producer's gaze with a critical gaze composed of academics and activists. By incorporating media images, Nottage investigates how the theoretical lens critics use to evaluate racial performance is muddled by analytical jargon that results in misrepresentations of art. In act 2, the viewer witnesses as critics apply their own theoretical frameworks onto films and television programs to unpack the deeper meaning of the performances. However, the result often obscures the significance of the performances, which results in comedic analyses that privilege the critics' own political perspectives. Both acts work together to challenge the viewer to acknowledge their own implicit views of race and critique how these assessments affect their understanding of racial performance.

Hollywood's Myth Making in *The Belle of New Orleans*

By the Way, Meet Vera Stark (*BTW*) begins with a dedication "in remembrance of Theresa Harris, Nina Mae McKinney, Mildred Washington and all the unsung *Black Divas of Early Hollywood*."[3] Although Nottage does not investigate the lives of real actresses in her play, she does investigate the realities of the experiences that Harris, McKinney, and Washington would have endured during the historical moment of the work. Act 1 is set during 1933 during the Great Depression. This era in American cinema featured problematic images of race on the big screen. Charlene Regester writes, "It is in mainstream or Hollywood films from before the 1960s that the form and function of the black actress can be seen as a shadow of the Other, with the Other in this regard referring to a leading White female actress/character. In many of these films, the black actress's principal function was—by contrast in language, costume, and behavior—to illuminate or aggrandize the virtue, beauty, morality, sexuality, sophistication, and other qualities embedded in the 'Whiteness' of the White female actress and character."[4] The depiction of Black women on screen focused on stereotypes and insisted on the women's subservience. At the time, the narratives told in Hollywood distorted relationships between members of differing races to uphold an image of White supremacy. The result of this strategy is a generation of films that reduce Blackness to the background to showcase White stars.

BTW is set in 1933, one year before the implementation of the Hays Code in Hollywood. Even before this period, there were regulations that policed what could and could not be seen on screen. Movies were an important part of American popular culture, and many religious and political groups considered them dangerous, because they believed that film could shape American values. In 1922, leaders in the film industry created the Motion Picture Producers and Distributors of America and selected William Harrison Hays for leadership to help protect the industry against a rise in censorship that was occurring across various states.[5] These states banned films or demanded that portions of films be deleted before they could be screened. This caused additional costs that were detrimental to profits within the industry. Because censorship bills had been approved in various states, movie makers decided to create a self-censoring code to help guide the creation of the films to avoid censorship and boycotts after the films were released. In 1934, the Production Code Administration was created to review scripts and films to ensure that they met the moral standards embedded within the code.[6] The code regulated subject matter, and "studios were encouraged to refrain from profanity, nudity, drug trafficking, and White slavery. When presenting mature issues such as criminal behavior, sexual relations and violence producers were [instructed] to remain tactful."[7]

One consequence of these censorship policies is that relationships between Black and White people could not be openly depicted within an accurate historical context. The code rationalized historical inaccuracy within film and whitewashed narratives by privileging singular perspectives in film. The result can be seen dramatized in Vera's career opportunities in Nottage's play. There are few options for Black actresses to play roles that highlight experiences crafted from a Black perspective. Consequently, Black actors are reduced to menial supporting characters. Vera's description of *The Belle of New Orleans* is one example of this. She characterizes the film as: "The story of a beautiful octoroon, who falls hopelessly in love with a White merchant. She contracts scarlet fever . . . and she's dying, but . . . but must alas pretend not to love the merchant in a selfless attempt to shield him from the truth about her race. . . . There's a big role in it for a lady's maid, Tilly. A real good honest-to-God part."[8] The description betrays the film's dubious premise. First, it presents the story of a mixed-race woman who is in love with a White man. However, the director wants to cast a White actress to play this role, because romantic interracial relationships are taboo. Susan Courtney notes that "the production code's sixth regulation on matters of 'sex' boldly declared: Miscegenation (sex relationship between the white and black races) is forbidden."[9] Second, the mixed-race woman is a tragic mulatto figure who denies her love to prevent her beau from facing the social stigma of loving her. Finally, her sickness and death symbolize the character's inability to fit neatly into White or Black society. The film's narrative explores different experiences of Blackness, yet the production of the film pushes the Black actors to the margins and casts Whiteness as the center. The film mirrors the social realities that Vera and her Black castmates face. Maryann Erigha suggests that "underrepresentation in the film industry undercuts rights to citizenship. . . . Assessing the level of representation in media is one method of gauging a group's access to cultural citizenship, which includes standard components such as voting rights and free speech but also the right to produce and be recognized in a nation's dominant myths, narratives, and images."[10] In *BTW*, Nottage explores how films reflect social norms on the screen by highlighting the way films are made. Vera is sidelined on screen and in real life. Her story emphasizes her attempt to work within a system governed by policies that are meant to erase her from the narrative of American life.

The racial dynamics of the film industry in the 1930s restricted the kinds of racial narratives available for production. Within this context, Nottage explores the strategies Black women utilized to work within a racist industry to perform their craft. Harvey Young sees *BTW* "as a passing narrative and, in a way, falls into a long tradition of literary, theatre, and film works that center on the challenges facing men and women who are racially indeterminate."[11] Although there is clearly an element of passing within the play, *BTW* goes beyond the conventions of typical passing narratives by considering all performances of Blackness in White spaces. There is a clear division between the impression of Blackness when Black characters are on the stage without their White counterparts. Nottage shows the audience nuanced Black performances by highlighting differences between the presentation of Blackness with or without a White presence. It is the presence of Whiteness that shapes Black performance throughout the play. When White people are present, Black actors operate in ways meant to appease White expectations while fulfilling the individual Black actor's goals. Nottage shows Black actors' perpetuating racial stereotypes in their performances but incorporates a subversive tone by foregrounding the agendas of individual Black characters throughout the play. Because there were few options for complex representations of Blackness within Hollywood at the time, the characters in this play perform various racial stereotypes to have an opportunity to be seen and heard on film. Gloria and Anna Mae adopt racial passing as a strategy to win roles, whereas Lottie and Vera adopt elements of minstrelsy to infiltrate the world of cinema. Nottage utilizes these characters' racial performances to demonstrate the strategies that some Black performers used to work in old Hollywood.

Nottage humanizes the Black women in her play by emphasizing their goals. Despite the racist environment they inhabit, they still desire to be creatives. In act 1, Vera is seen through her relationships with her roommates Anna Mae and Lottie. It is the possibility to perform on film that motivates the women throughout the play. However, the politics of the film industry results in limited opportunities for the women to achieve their desires. *The Belle of New Orleans* presents a chance for these actors to move beyond the background and be seen and heard on screen.

Vera: Well, sugar, there's work to be had. W-O-R-K! You hear what I'm saying? WORK! Every tap dancing fool and two-bit hustler's been talking about it . . . wake up, honey.

Lottie: Yeah, yeah. I believe it when I see it. How many times have I heard that damn refrain?

Vera: Turn up your nose, but I'll put it this way, a couple of the Negroes actually get to say something other than "yes' um" and "no 'um."[12]

Vera's explanation conveys the significance of the film to the community of actors on the back lots at the time. They all are vying for the few roles available. *The Belle of New Orleans* presents them with a chance to do more than serve.

This film promises to be a big break for the Black actors lucky enough to get cast, but Lottie explains that talent is not what studio insiders are looking for when casting coveted roles: "You gotta be high yella mellow or look like you crawled outta Mississippi cotton patch to get work in this town. So here I am, or should I say here is, seven years later trying to eat my way into some work, looking like someone's mammy and the closest I've gotten to the pictures is sitting in the back row of the cinema."[13] Lottie argues that Black actors must visually fit within the narrow confines of acceptable Black presence on the film screen. Her discussion of skin color asserts that directors display colorist ideas when casting Black talent. An actor must be very light skinned or dark skinned to portray the few menial roles available. Anyone in between these polar representations of Blackness has a hard time succeeding. However, the reality of these limitations does not prevent Lottie from trying to be cast. She attempts to fulfill the image of the mammy by overeating and changing her natural shape.

Lottie's physical transformation exhibits a criticism of racial performance in Hollywood. Lottie must conform to an image of Blackness that is ahistorical and represents what bell hooks calls "a creature of white imagination."[14] hooks describes the mythologized image of the Black mammy from slavery as follows: "First and foremost asexual and consequently she had to be fat (preferably obese). . . . Her greatest virtue was of course her love for white folk whom she willingly and passively served. The mammy image was portrayed with affection by whites because it epitomized the ultimate sexist-racist vision of ideal black womanhood—complete submission to the will of whites.?"[15] Lottie's physical transformation shows how Black bodies are shaped by White ideals. The tragedy of her character's performance is that to achieve her goal of film stardom, she must assume the posture of Black womanhood that is most palatable to White audiences. The mammy in American film is divorced from the reality of slave nurses and from the sexual trauma they experienced.

The image of the mammy on screen is meant to entertain White audiences, but Lottie's experience emphasizes the weight that Black actors bear as a result. Her racial performance extends beyond the world of films, as the transformation she has undergone is not a costume that she can remove. Through Lottie's character, Nottage dramatizes how racial performances can shape our reality. Lottie's experience of racism in casting encourages her to adapt to her environment. As she attempts to achieve her goal of acting in film, she realizes that there are few roles for Black women who look like her. She chooses to gain weight and enacts a gendered racialized character to subvert the barriers she faces as an actress. The cost of this racial performance is staggering, but Nottage does not critique Lottie for her decision. Instead, she uses Lottie's narrative to critique an industry that manipulates Black womanhood to advance racist ahistorical narratives.

As Black actresses Vera and Lottie plot their auditions for the movie, Gloria Mitchell also attempts to audition by inviting the film's producer and director to her house. During this party, Lottie and Vera work as domestics serving Gloria and the filmmakers. While Gloria entertains her guests, the production team quarrels about the direction of the film. Central to that quarrel is a discussion of the purpose of the film. The director, Maximillian Van Oster, claims that he has a unique vision for the presentation of the South, and, through *The Belle of New Orleans*, he envisions an opportunity for realism. Maximillian describes his vision of the film as:

> Thoroughly authentic. If *The Belle of New Orleans* is like every other film that we've seen, then vhat is the point. It is time for cinema to take bold new leap. It is time to capture the truth. For instance, I vant the Negroes to be real, to be Negroes of the earth, I vant to feel their struggle, the rhythm of their language, I vant actors that . . . no, I don't vant actors, I vant people. Negroes who felt the burden of hard unmerciful labor. I vant to see hundred years of oppression in the hunch of their shoulders.[16]

Nottage uses humor to expose Maximillian's racist views of Black southerners. His description of Black life is reductive and assumes that the center of the Black experience in the United States is struggle. He negates the complexities of the Black experience and asserts a monolithic interpretation of Black life. His earnest tone adds to the humor of the moment. His ignorance of African-American people dehumanizes them and flattens the totality of their varied experiences, substituting their complex realities with his narrow vision of their existence. The foundation of his argument for an authentic depiction of African-American southern life on screen assumes a posture of paternalism. Maximillian's obliviousness of the everyday realities of African Americans in the twentieth century manifests through his inability to conceive of a difference in the lives of Black people during the Depression versus the antebellum era. Finally, he undervalues the skills necessary to perform in movies when he advocates for African Americans who are not actors to portray characters from the Antebellum era.

In opposition, the producer of the film, Mr. Slasvick, is concerned about the cost of the project and seeks to steer the film toward profit. "I want romance, and maybe a couple of musical numbers. If I wanted a critique of antebellum New Orleans I'd have checked a book out of the library."[17] Slasvick's impression of filmmaking focuses on entertainment. He fears that any realistic depiction of slavery in the South would be censured in both the South and the North. His arguments suggest that there exists a separation between realism and amusement. From his impression, his target audience does not want to be educated about the historical realities of racism. Instead, "People want to laugh, they want to cry and they want a little sing-and-dance in between. And I don't think that's so fucking awful. But the one thing they don't want is to feel bad about themselves . . . people need the past, need their history to seem heroic, glorious and romantic. That is what we do, erase their pain for ninety minutes."[18]

Although seemingly arguing different perspectives, both Maximillian and Slasvick represent racism in the film industry. Maximillian wants to exploit Black trauma for profit, and Slasvick seeks to create a mythologized image of the South that avoids the reality of slavery's devastating impact on Black lives. It is within this context that Vera, Lottie, Gloria, and Anna Mae perform informal auditions for various parts in *The Belle of New Orleans* during Gloria's party. Gloria and Anna Mae's performances invoke racial passing. Harvey Young suggests "Nottage presents four African-American women, two of whom (Gloria and Anna Mae) 'play' non-black, while the other two (Vera and Lottie) enact an extreme caricature of Blackness. Together, their acts stretch not only the possibilities of Blackness but also the fragility of racial assumptions."[19] Throughout the play, Gloria Mitchell passes as White. However, at the end of the play, Nottage reveals that Gloria and Vera are cousins who grew up together in Brooklyn. Through racial passing, Gloria has achieved great success as a White starlet, but this new film offers her an opportunity to achieve critical success. Nottage plays with the audience's understanding of race by having a Black woman's performance of Whiteness go unnoticed by White people. This adds a level of humor to the piece, because the audience is in on the joke. Maximillian wants to cast a White woman to play the "octoroon" character Miss Marie because of miscegenation rules, but he is actually considering a Black woman for the role.

Throughout the play, Anna Mae dates White men with power and passes for White or some exotic other. Vera learns that Anna Mae has been courting the director of the upcoming film at Gloria's house when she shows up as Maximillian's date. At Gloria's house, Anna begins an impromptu rehearsal. She passes as Brazilian and performs an exoticized hypersexualized persona. Her ploy utilizes sexual overtures to flirt her way into a role in the film. When the men leave the room to discuss the film after a moment of disagreement, Vera challenges Anna Mae:

> Vera: You're playing way out of your league, honey.
> Anna Mae: Ain't I though. It's only cuz my playmates don't care for the games I play.
> Vera: How long do you think you can keep up the front?
> Anna Mae: Oh, he's buying what I'm selling, even if it ain't the real thing. Trust me, in the bedroom a horny joe ain't so particular about the accent.
> Vera: You are one devious dame.
> Anna Mae: Oh, grow up, everyone in this town has an angle. Listen here, I'm gonna get me a role in this picture, and the studio ain't gonna have a lot to say about it.[20]

Anna Mae defies the traditional casting system by pursuing a sexual relationship with the director, but she does submit to the casting couch, which undermines her agency. She manipulates him by passing as Brazilian, but the whole time she is aware of the game she is playing. Ultimately, she is willing to utilize her sexuality to subvert the system to gain access to the big screen. Vera chastises Anna Mae, but Anna Mae balks at her disapproval by reminding her that everyone is performing in some way. She does not apologize for her behavior, because she does not find her behavior questionable. Nottage utilizes Anna Mae's conviction regarding her decision to pass as a symbol for subversion. Anna Mae did not create the racist industry she works within or the racial policies that govern the system. She has found loopholes within the system that she willingly utilizes. Her future career in cinema attests to the convincing nature of her performance and the malleable nature of race in Hollywood. Blackness and Whiteness are not static. Black characters perform Whiteness and exoticism with the same level of success as their performances of Blackness. Through these varied racial performances, Nottage questions the socially constructed nature of race as Anna Mae slips in and out of Blackness for her benefit.

Although Vera questions Anna Mae, she soon begins to perform racial stereotypes to receive favor from Maximillian. After hearing Maximillian's conversation with Slasvick regarding his desire for authenticity "Vera and Lottie hunch their shoulders, continuing to morph. Vera, seeing an opportunity, slowly and in the character of a slave, crosses to freshen his drink. Her gait is slow, posture deferential."[21] Much like Anna Mae, Vera adopts a new posture separate from the real life she leads for commercial gain. Vera adopts a southern vernacular to audition for the role of Tilly. As Maximillian becomes more interested in her performance, she concocts a dramatic story to support her act.

> Vera: (*Lying*): My mama died in childbirth cuz there wasn't no doctor there to birth me proper, and you see my pappy wuz a blues man, and he guitar was the onliest thing he luv. My pappy dun own heself a joke joint. . . . And as a chil' I workedid dere cuz he couldn' afford no other help. Nah, suh. I work-did like a grown woman, though I was nuthin' but a chil'. I dun seen plenty of ugly things, things no chil' need see. But my pappy was a good man, but, mister, sometime in de South a good man hafta do ugly things to survive.[22]

Vera's performance plays to Maximillian's reductive view of Blackness and reveals the price she is willing to pay to achieve success in Hollywood.

Her performance signals a change in Vera's character. Throughout the first act, Vera discusses what it means to be an artist. Whereas Lottie has become cynical regarding the Hollywood system, Vera initially remains hopeful. However, when she creates a false narrative about her supposed southern upbringing, she crosses a line she did not know existed for her and immediately feels energized. "I actually did something I vowed I'd never do, and I did it so easily it frightened me. And I got to thinking about what I'd be willing to do have a taste of what Gloria's got."[23] Instead of remorse for adopting stereotypes to win the role of Tilly, she feels ambitious. Unlike Anna Mae, she acknowledges that this performance represents a change in direction for her, and she hopes that the risk she has taken will guarantee her future success. Although Vera imagines that she is different from Gloria, Lottie, and Anna Mae, her actions suggest that Vera is willing to sacrifice her integrity to gain the role of Tilly, like her friends.

In act I, Nottage avoids judging the Black actresses for the choices they make to survive the racist and sexist system they work within. Instead, she crafts a historically believable context that presents the actors with various choices. The actors must make decisions that impact their lives on and off screen. Nottage presents Vera's agenda to succeed in Hollywood and exposes the obstacles that stand in the way of her success. By shifting a marginalized character to the center of a narrative about old Hollywood, Nottage explores the subject of racism in the film industry by exposing the limited opportunities for success for Black actors. By centering Vera's narrative, Nottage poses important questions regarding the entertainment business. What does it mean to be successful in film as a Black actor? What consequences do actors face when they perform stereotypical representations of Blackness? Act 1 depicts actors at the beginning of their careers who are willing to make sacrifices to achieve stardom. Act 2 shifts course and reflects on the outcome of these choices for the individual actors and the legacy of the choices they make. Whereas Nottage refuses to judge Vera and her peers, the contemporary scholars in act 2 critique the performances on and off screen. These critics evaluate Vera and her performance as Tilly as symbolic of her place in Hollywood.

How Critics Shape the Audience's View of Vera/Tilly

Act 2 begins with a screening of *The Belle of New Orleans* at a symposium in 2003. At the symposium, the final scene from the film is played and presents the death of Gloria's character, Marie. This scene also informs the audience of the outcome of the lively auditions from the first act. Gloria, Vera, Anna Mae, and Lottie were all cast in the film, which initially suggests their collective success. However, act 2 reveals the divergent paths that Vera and Gloria traveled after this groundbreaking moment. The symposium, titled "Rediscovering Vera Stark, the Legacy of *The Belle of New Orleans*," investigates the professional and personal life of Vera Stark.[24] Specifically, the symposium presents a robust discussion between three critics, Carmen Levy-Green, professor of media and gender studies; Afua Assata Ejobo, journalist and poet; and filmmaker Herb Forrester, regarding the significance of Vera Stark's performance in the film and speculates about her last years. During the panel's discussion, video from Vera's last televised interview, from a 1973 episode of the fictionalized *The Brad Donavan Show*, is screened. Nottage juxtaposes media from film and television into the panel's discussion. Soyica Diggs Colbert asserts that Nottage's use of archival film and television sources within the panel serves "as a corrective to historical misapprehensions of blackness . . . [that] draws from the black feminist historiographical practice of troubling what qualifies as historical."[25] Diggs Colbert compares the work of the panel to "Alice Walker's recuperation of Zora Neale Hurston" in Walker's *In Search of Our Mothers' Gardens*.[26] In this way, Diggs Colbert asserts a comparison between Hurston and Stark. The comparison alludes to Vera's importance in art but also suggests her fall from grace and eventual erasure from history. The panel seeks to do corrective work by reclaiming Vera through a critical discussion regarding the significance of her performance as Tilly and the trials she faced as a Black actress working within the racist and sexist power structures of the film industry in the first half of the twentieth century.

The guiding questions that the panel discuss are as follows: "What happened to Vera Stark? In late 1973 she mysteriously disappeared. Why? Did she take her own life as it's been suggested in Grandford Ellis's brilliant book *Subverting Blackness*? Or was she cannibalized by our culture?"[27] As the panelists consider these questions, Nottage encourages the audience to witness how academic analysis of film and television impacts the critical discussion of the art. The symposium reveals how critical analyses of artists and the art they produce are framed through the lens of critics' perspectives. These perspectives can skew the artists' original intent. The interactions during act 2, scene 2, expose how critics apply their unique perspectives to a text. Often connected to a theoretical lens, these perspectives can impact the way the artwork and the artists are perceived by audience members. Nottage emphasizes the interplay between artists and critics and offers a critique of the latter's work. According to Diggs Colbert, "*By the Way, Meet Vera Stark* reveals how theorizing the performance of blackness must function differently from theorizing the performance of normative identity, because theories of black performance must account for the determining ways in which racial fantasies shape Black identity."[28] She asserts that evaluating performances of Blackness and evaluating Black performers requires a nuanced critical gaze. In act 2, Nottage points to the limitations of critical conversations about Black performance on the stage and screen through the panel. Through the dynamic interactions between the panelists, she asserts how critical discussions often blur the lines between the performer and the performance. This creates a problem within the critical discussion, as the characters are conflated with the actors at work. Nottage calls for a rethinking of how performance theories should be applied to works through the misunderstandings and political posturing the audience views within the panel. When discussing Vera, the critics make assumptions about her as an individual and conflate her performance of Tilly with Vera the person. This is a mistake. The audience realizes this through their intimate understanding of Vera from act 1. However, the panel is important because critical conversations about the art and the artist promotes continued interest in the artist.

In "Zora Neale Hurston: A Cautionary Tale and a Partisan View," Alice Walker performs the type of intersectional critical analysis that the panelists individually attempt to recover Vera Stark. Walker notes that her analysis of Hurston represents a partisan view through her affinity for Hurston's life and work. However, she models the kind of separate evaluative experience that Nottage contends is necessary when critiquing Black artists. Walker claims:

> Having committed myself to Zora's work, loving it, in fact, I became curious as to what others had written about her. This was, for the young,

> impressionable, barely begun writer I was, a mistake. After reading the misleading, deliberately belittling, inaccurate, and generally irresponsible attacks on her work and her life by almost everyone, I became for a time paralyzed with confusion and fear. . . . Eventually, however, I discovered that I repudiate and despise the kind of criticism that intimidates rather than instructs the young; and I dislike fear, especially in myself. I did then what fear rarely fails to force me to do: I fought back. I began to fight for Zora and her work; for what I knew was good must not be lost to us.[29]

The members of the panel are like Walker in their affinity for Stark, but their opinions of her work and her responsibility for the images she helps create in *The Belle of New Orleans* vary. After viewing an argument between Gloria and Vera from the talk show, the panelists attempt to synthesize the tensions between her performance and persona.

> Herb: Vera may have been a promising actress, but over the years she has presented such a contradictory narrative of self. It's hard to say who she really was.
>
> Carmen: Yes, but Vera believed she was breathing fresh life into painful stereotypes, but ultimately she was . . . denied agency // that's what I hear echoed in the footage and particularly in her relationship to Gloria Mitchell.
>
> Herb: Even so, the Vera I know was aiding and abetting Hollywood's // distortion of history.
>
> Afua: Yo, my girl battled writers, // directors who had no clue and little interest in who she was—
>
> Herb: We all agree Vera was simply breathtaking in *The Belle of New Orleans*, but ultimately she was just another shucking, jiving, // fumbling, mumbling, laughing, shuffling, pancake-making mammy in the kitchen.
>
> Afua: Stop! NO! My girl may have been many things, but she refused to be reduced to an image on the screen. // She says so much.
>
> Herb: Theories! Rumors! Conjecture! I don't give a goddamn! The images remain problematic. And those images are indelible, and they can't simply be apologized away—
>
> Carmen: But we have to actively engage with them, listen to them and understand why they exist, and perhaps what the performer was attempting to tell us about the ethos of the time. . . .[30]

Each critic's theoretical perspective informs their analysis. Herb's film background results in a hyperfocus on the film while negating the historical context of the system in which Vera worked. Afua's background as a performer and lesbian frames her interpretation of Vera's defiance on and off screen. While Carmen's background in gender studies and media studies afford her the theoretical framework to combine an understanding of the systems of power that shaped Vera's experience of racial and gender barriers. She represents a synthesis between Afua's and Herb's perspectives by evaluating the film and Vera's life within the historical context of the time. Nottage exposes flaws within critical perspectives that refuse to acknowledge the historical situations that artists work within and that art reflects. By removing a conversation about the racist and sexist elements throughout Hollywood's industry, critics miss an opportunity to have a complex evaluation of the film. The tone of the symposium does not fully consider the limitations within which Black female actors worked during that time. By focusing on Vera and her choices, the conversation further mitigates the actions of producers and directors to perpetuate stereotypes on screen. Carmen's perspective identifies the tragedy in this approach by addressing the power dynamics at play off screen in *The Belle of New Orleans*.

Conclusion

Nottage explores the function of critiques of racial performance throughout the play. Through the panel's criticisms of Vera, Nottage poses questions about the responsibility of artists and critics alike. Walker asserts that the work of critics of Black artists and Black art is specific: "We are a people. A people do not throw their geniuses away. And if they are thrown away, it is our duty as artists and as witnesses for the future to collect them again for the sake of our children, and if necessary, bone by bone."[31] Walker clarifies a part of the Black feminist critical agenda that Carmen and Afua apply differently throughout the second act. Both women are aware that the specific subject position within the historical context of *The Brad Donavan Show* and *The Belle of New Orleans* reflects a system of oppression that Vera struggled against privately and professionally throughout her life. To critique an African-American female performer and her performances requires a nuanced understanding of the expectations of racial performance in media. These expectations cannot be divorced from art or the artists working within a specific time frame. Furthermore, the play explores how these expectations are subverted by Vera, yet Herb continues to blame Vera for the Mammy archetype reflected in Tilly. The questions he asks regarding what happened to Vera and what responsibility she bears for Tilly are too narrow to answer fully in the symposium. Additionally, the questions suggest a responsibility that is not Vera's alone to carry.

Vera's performances in the film and on the talk show provide a point of entry into an analysis of a larger system of representation. Why were films like *The Belle of New Orleans* ever made? What were the goals in crafting ahistorical narratives about a part of southern history? How have those narratives shaped contemporary understandings of race and gender? Nottage's play evokes these questions and others as she presents Vera and her performances. A part of Vera's legacy is that her performance represents the tension of a figure struggling to perform Blackness in venues that distort representations of race and gender for financial gain. Movies and television shows are not often realistic, and Vera is seemingly punished for the roles she played because they appear to represent submissive images of Blackness. Nottage shows in her play that African-American artists are aware of expectations of racial and gender performances. Their understanding of the expectations of primarily White audiences does not make them responsible for those perspectives. To answer the question "What happened to Vera Stark?" is to consider the spaces available for her throughout her life. Vera's performance of Tilly deserves critical analysis because it represents a digital archive of American values. The narrative surrounding the production and the interplay between the actors provides a colorful backstory into the creation of the film. Furthermore, the play offers the audience an opportunity to contemplate the work and the artists as products of a specific time and place. To fully understand the significance of Vera's performance and her eventual disappearance from the screen requires a frank inquiry into the values that confined her throughout her performance and life.

CHAPTER 8

Anticipating the Political Divide in *Sweat*

With *Sweat*, Lynn Nottage became the only African-American female playwright to win two Pulitzer Prizes for drama. Commissioned by the Oregon Shakespeare Festival, *Sweat* premiered in Ashland, Oregon, on July 29, 2015. Both productions were directed by Kate Whoriskey, and the Broadway production featured a diverse cast of actors, including Michelle Wilson, Lance Coadie Williams, Miriam Shor, Will Pullen, John Earl Jelks, Johanna Day, James Colby, Khris Davis, and Carlo Alban, portraying factory workers in Reading, Pennsylvania.[1] By the time *Sweat* premiered on Broadway in November 2016, many critics appraised Nottage's powerful work about the connection between the 2008 economic collapse as a prescient play that connected the consequences of the 2008 recession to the growing political divide in the United States, which culminated in the election of President of Donald J. Trump.

However, Nottage did not set out to make a political play. A friend's personal crisis inspired her to investigate the economic problems that many middle-class Americans were facing. In an interview with Sarah Crompton from *The Guardian*, Nottage stated:

> I got an email from a friend sharing the fact that for a period of time she had been completely and absolutely broke. She was someone I knew quite well and saw regularly. I felt horrible that I had no idea she was struggling. The next morning, we had a long conversation that coincided with the beginning of the first week of the Occupy Wall Street protest against economic inequality. So, these two middle-aged women went down there and chanted. Nothing changed, but at least she knew she was not alone. To me, Occupy Wall Street raised a lot of questions that were not answered. That

> put me out on the street to figure out how economic stagnation was shifting the American narrative and how so many people who had so thoroughly invested in the American dream found themselves broadsided.[2]

This personal crisis created a space for exploring America's economic landscape. Wayne Duggan asserted that "The Great Recession of 2008 to 2009 was the worst economic downturn in the U.S. since the Great Depression. Domestic product declined 4.3%, the unemployment rate doubled to more than 10%, home prices fell roughly 30% and at its worst point, the S&P 500 was down 57% from its highs. What started as a classic tale of greed and deregulation ended in a global crisis that caused six million households to lose their homes. As a result, unprecedented reforms and bailouts were implemented that are still in place today."[3]

Nottage's research led her to Reading, Pennsylvania. Once an industrial giant, the collapse of manufacturing jobs crippled the city's once flourishing economy. In 2011, Reading ranked as the number one impoverished US city according to the Census Bureau.[4] The global economic collapse of 2007–2008 altered Reading. Workers who dedicated their lives to companies suddenly found that their jobs were disappearing. Nottage created three projects from her research in Reading: *Sweat*; *This Is Reading*, a multimodal art display she created with her husband filmmaker, Tony Gerber; and *Clyde's* (2021).[5] This three-work cycle focuses on the people of the city and their commitment to work. The city serves as a microcosm of the economic and political problems evident in the United States. As the middle class began to dwindle, hardworking Americans felt dismissed and looked for a scapegoat to blame for their current personal problems. In *Sweat*, Nottage examines this phenomenon in Reading.

When factories outsource their manufacturing to countries without labor unions and fewer regulations, American workers struggle to survive. Nottage documents how these issues destroy communities and relationships. The play observes several workers at a local steel tubing plant factory, Olstead's. Jessie, Cynthia, Tracey, are a group of friends who have history in the community and the company. Jason and Chris represent the younger generations of workers. As the stability of their jobs is questioned, each character struggles with an uncertain future. Stan and Brucie, former factory workers, serve as a reminder that companies rarely treat their loyal workers fairly. Finally, Oscar, a first-generation American, attempts to enter the old boys' club that previously locked out Hispanic workers from union jobs. His presence complicates the narrative and confirms the seeds of racism that later grow into the foundation of political discontent. Through the complex relationships in Reading, Nottage investigates global issues underlying the economic crisis and sheds light its origins.

Sweat takes place in 2000 as well as in 2008, alternating between both years to show the economic and social collapse of Reading. The play is framed through the reflections of two characters, Chris and Jason. They allude to their troubled past as they conduct required meetings with their probation officer, Evan. From the beginning of the play, Nottage hints at a turbulent past that results in an event that sends both characters to jail. She refrains from disclosing the specific criminal activity that the two participate in until the end of the play. However, the tone established in the initial scenes of the play, set in 2008, is a somber one, full of regret and loss during Jason's and Chris's respective meetings with their probation officer. Nottage's manipulation of time in the play hints at the political landscape during the era in which the play was first performed. The play predates the 2016 US presidential election of Donald J. Trump, yet the discourse within the play predicts his election. Richard S. Conley explains "during the 2016 presidential campaign and well into his first two years in office, Trump vigorously celebrated ordinary Americans—the middle class, blue-collar workers, manual laborers, and farmers. Pledging an economic renewal that included the return of manufacturing jobs. . . ."[6] Trump utilized the discontent bred from a loss of economic stability in the labor sector. Nottage dramatizes the experiences of some of these workers in *Sweat*.

Sweat explores the various factors that combined to create the economic collapse of 2008. One business that was at the center of the economic depression was the auto industry. As business owners sought bailouts from the federal government, they betrayed dedicated employees by shipping their secure manufacturing jobs to overseas locations that guaranteed cheaper labor. As a result, American manufacturing jobs plummeted and unemployment rose. The workers felt slighted and left behind. Politicians like President Trump understood this population's weakness and manipulated them by preying on their fears of being replaced by foreign workers. Trump capitalized on their anger and leveraged it into a successful presidential run. In *Sweat*, Nottage evaluates this population by considering the connection between their work and identity. When companies abuse a loyal base of workers, tensions rise as they struggle to determine who is to blame for their change in status.

The Beginning of the End

The relationships in *Sweat* drive the action. Nottage depicts a close-knit community where generations of workers have loyally worked in factories. These factories gave the characters a false sense of belonging to something greater, but their disposability becomes evident as rumors of layoffs circulate through the community. A trio of old friends, Jessie, Tracey, and Cynthia, visit a neighborhood bar run by Stan. This community watering hole is a place where the women come for drinks after work and for birthday celebrations. Stan is a former factory worker who sustained a serious injury that took him off the factory floor. As the manager of this local bar, he provides his patrons with insight into the political climate by warning them of tensions on the horizon. During a conversation with the group, Stan cautions them to pay more attention to the news because factories are closing more and more. "You saw what happened over at Clemmons Technologies. No one saw that coming. Right? You could wake up tomorrow and all your jobs are in Mexico."[7] The group seems hesitant to believe that their company, Olstead, could ship their jobs away because of the company's long-standing presence within the community. Additionally, as members of a strong labor union, the trio overestimates their power. Throughout *Sweat*, each member of the friend group is forced to reevaluate their relationship to Olstead and their position within the community. Their jobs have long been a source of pride and stability, but the company's impending layoffs produces chaos at work and at the bar.

Jessie

Jessie consistently tries to keep the peace within her friend group. Her attempts to salvage the relationship resemble other failures in her personal and professional life. When introduced at Tracey's birthday party in act 1, she is presented as an alcoholic. Her alcoholism throughout the play hints at Jessie's dissatisfaction with her life. At Tracey's party, Jessie picks a fight with Stan after he refuses to sell her drinks. Their quarrel exposes her marital problems.

> Jessie: You can't talk to me that way. My husband—
> Stan: You mean your ex.
> Jessie: All I gotta do is make one phone call and he'll wipe that fucking smile off your face.
> Stan: Yeah, go ahead. Here, use my phone. Wake up his beautiful young wife, what's her name again, Tiffany?[8]

Jessie uses alcohol to numb the pain of her current situation. She is middle-aged, unmarried, and facing an impending strike at work. She drinks to avoid addressing her problems. At another celebration, Cynthia reminds Jessie of her past dreams. However, Jessie has not fulfilled her potential. She has devoted her life to a marriage that ended unsuccessfully. Similarly, she has remained a loyal employee to Olstead from the time she finished high school. As a teenager, she dreamed of traveling the world, but her dedication to the company did not allow her to fulfill her ambition. Consequently, Jessie's dedication to Olstead has come at the price of her personal goals.

In act 2, Jessie reminisces about her unfulfilled dreams. "That was so long ago. We were gonna do Alaska, camp, live clean, you know, and save enough money to get to India. Live in an ashram for a while, then bum along the hippie trail. Istanbul, Tehran, Kandahar, Kabul, Peshawar, Lashore, Kathmandu. Places. . . . That was the plan,"[9] Instead, she worked. Through Jessie, Nottage considers the cost of labor in the United States. Jessie represents a generation of workers who depended on their place of employment to take care of them. She leveraged her future ambitions to travel and experience the world for the promise of stability. As Olstead prepares to lay off seasoned workers and bring in temporary employees, Jessie considers her life and her regrets. At Jessie's party, Chris asks her about her life. "I guess, I wish. . . . I had gotten to see the world. You know, left Berks, if only for a year. That's what I regret. Not the work, I regret the fact that for a little while it seemed like, I don't know there was possibility. I think about that Jessie on the other side of the world and what she woulda seen."[10] Her words do not correspond with her actions in the play. Jessie's perpetual drunken state emphasizes her unhappiness. Jessie does not blame the dedication required by her employer for her inability to travel. She tries to compartmentalize her despair by separating a lifetime of work from her personal failures. Unable to reconcile her personal choices with the requirements of employment, Jessie chooses oblivion through alcoholism. She tries to escape her reality by drinking to excess. When she awakens, she begins the process all over again. She cleans herself up and clocks in on time for her shift.

Jessie's experience at Olstead is a cautionary tale. She bought into the American fallacy that hard work ensures success, and her life counters the myth of the American dream. Instead, her life resembles a nightmare. The deeper meaning she sought as a young woman is swept away through the repetition in her present life. Jessie lacks vigor and aim. Even before the strike and layoffs, Jessie is a depressing character. She represents the toll that a lifetime of work has on the body and soul. M. Scott Phillips contends that the play's "central issue is identity and crises of identity precipitated by disrupted narratives of American exceptionalism and progress, two of our most cherished mythic spaces."[11] Phillips's claim underscores the emotional debt that laborers face through their dedication to companies. Jessie's narrative emphasizes that laborers are not ensured comfort and wealth, despite their efforts. Jessie fights an unwinnable battle at work and within her private life. As conflicts arise within the group, she seeks to restore the balance but fails. As the situation at work degenerates, her personal relationships suffer. Ultimately,

Jessie is unable to successfully address the tensions within her group of friends, save her marriage, or salvage her position at work. Her hard work has not resulted in the stable life promised to generations of Americans. Unable to solve these problems, she dissolves into her pint at the end of the bar.

Cynthia

Cynthia's journey in *Sweat* is tumultuous. As an African-American woman, her position at Olstead has been difficult. In addition to dealing with sexism, she faces racist attitudes from her colleagues and superiors throughout her twenty-four years of experience at the plant. Nevertheless, Cynthia is defined by her determination to succeed. Like Jessie, she has endured an unsuccessful marriage with ex-husband Brucie, who once worked at a neighboring factory but experienced a mental breakdown after the company locked out their workers. His breakdown results in his ongoing dependence on drugs, and his addiction ruined their marriage. Although Cynthia still loves her husband, she chooses to relinquish that relationship because of his behavior. Her response to the failure of her marriage contrasts greatly with Jessie's. Cynthia is angry, but she rejects substances as a strategy to manage her pain. She has experienced firsthand the damage that addiction can cause. Cynthia decides to pour her energy into her job to find solace. At work, Cynthia achieves success through a positive reputation as a hard worker. Her hard work positions her for upward mobility, but her promotion soon threatens other important relationships in her life.

Initially, Cynthia holds the same position as her friends, Jessie and Tracey. She works on the factory floor as a prototypical blue-collar worker. Unlike her friends, she faced difficulty gaining entrance into the position because, at the time, the labor union upheld racist policies that prevented the entrance of Black workers into the union. Therefore, when she begins to work at Olstead, she feels pride for challenging racist standards. Decades of hard work provide an opportunity for a promotion to a managerial position. If earned, Cynthia would be the first factory worker to "make it off the floor." In act 1, Tracey and other workers vie for the position, but Cynthia wins the job. Her transition from coworker to supervisor proves difficult for the friend group. Initially, Cynthia faces a racist backlash because of her promotion. Jessie claims "Tracey's been going around town whispering that the only reason Cynthia got the job is cuz she's black."[12] Tracey's behavior worsens as Olstead begins to use divisive practices to break the labor union and lower the costs of production. Many of the workers view a strike as the only way to resist this maneuver.

As a manager, Cynthia is privy to the political maneuvers that the company is willing to engage in to ensure the workers' defeat. She warns them of what's to come:

Cynthia: It ain't gonna be easy. I can tell you how it's gonna play out. They're gonna ask for everyone to take a pay cut to save jobs. Sixty percent. . . . They're gonna ask for concessions on your benefits package next. I'm being straight. No bullshit. They're gonna ask you for more hours. They will give you a little bit of room for negotiation, and then they'll wait until your breaking point, at which point you'll be convinced that you've had a small victory. . . . You're dealing with vipers. The games changed! They'll kick you out and once they get you out, they're not gonna let you back in.[13]

Just as Cynthia has achieved her goal of moving beyond the factory floor, her new position puts her in conflict with her old friends. Cynthia's position provides her with inside information that she shares with the group to help them prepare for the battle that lies before them. However, instead of understanding the complicated position that they face, they lash out at Cynthia, accusing her of treachery. Because she is in a position of authority, she becomes an easy target for their criticisms. Cynthia's ascension to management fractures her friend group and stresses her relationship with her son, Chris. She bemoans her position to Stan: "I thought they'd take the damn deal. You think I'm happy about this? I locked out my own son. My own son. I saw the hurt on his face."[14] Cynthia is in a lose-lose situation. Although she was promoted, her position seems unstable. She even wonders whether the promotion was a maneuver by upper management to create a scapegoat for the changes and strike that they would initiate with their workers.

Cynthia's struggles in *Sweat* suggest several problems within a capitalist system. Companies dehumanize their workers by valuing costs over relationships. Beverly Andrews notes that "the play starkly demonstrates what happens when the world's richest country has an ever-increasing population trapped in an endless cycle of poverty, simply because they are now viewed as disposable."[15] Workers who invested generations of families into an organization often fail to see the benefit of their investments. When companies undervalue the loyal productivity of longtime workers compared with quick profits, they destabilize community trust by fracturing the connection between businesses and the people that serve them. Ultimately, Olstead has no intention of maintaining the factory in Reading. Before the company departs, it uses deceptive practices to minimize the amount of money owed to employees from pensions and other benefits. Olstead's political maneuvering contributes to the fractured relationships in the play. Moreover, the economic disparity that the characters endure in 2008 is a direct result of the policies enacted in 2000 to ensure company profit.

Tracey

Nottage works hard to humanize Tracey and the people she represents. Despite the decades of friendship Tracey shares with Cynthia, their conflict at work boils over into racist stereotypes. In an interview with Rob Weinert-Kendt, Nottage reflects on how the interviews she conducted with steel workers in Reading who had been laid off affected her view of the connection between the rise in White supremacy and the sagging economy. "But sitting in a room with these unemployed men . . . what surprised me was my ability to empathize with people who I always thought were on the other side of the divide. When you interview black and Latino folks, there is a narrative that has existed for the last 50 years of being sort of disaffected from the culture. But I sat in rooms with middle-aged white men and heard them speaking like young black men in America—they feel disenfranchised, disaffected."[16] White workers in Reading were frustrated because they felt that they were being left behind. Their Black and Latino counterparts have experienced obstacles with manufacturing jobs, but the economic downturn of 2008 highlighted how White workers faced instability in the job market. This feeling of not belonging after generations of privilege manifested in negative ways. The stark absence of community they felt after layoffs and shifts in the job market encouraged some more vulnerable individuals to seek out a new community in which to voice their complaints and frustrations. Nottage's interviews provide a context for understanding Tracey's behavior. It would be easy to dismiss Tracey's response to Cynthia's promotion as the ravings of a bigot, but her conversations with various characters throughout the play expose a deeply hurt woman who is struggling to understand her identity within the shifting landscape of her community.

Empathy is the guiding term that Nottage invokes in her attempt to make sense of the burgeoning White supremacists she interviewed in Reading. In *Sweat*, Nottage explores Tracey's slow decline into White supremacist rants as she attempts to rationalize how she was passed over for the managerial job. In act 1, scene 4, Tracey explains her initial beliefs about Cynthia's promotion to Oscar. "It's a fact. That's how things are going. And I'm not prejudice, I say, you are who you are, you know? I'm cool with everyone. But, I mean . . . c'mon . . . you guys coming over here, you can get a job faster than. . . ."[17] The irony of utilizing racist tropes when speaking to a first-generation Columbian American reveals Tracey's lack of insight regarding her racial privilege. To provide Oscar with context, she begins by denouncing racist ideology. For Tracey, the perception of racism is more harmful than the reality of the impact that casual racism has on people of color daily. She says that she is not prejudiced, but her statements suggest the opposite. Tracey undermines Cynthia's experience and qualifications to justify her reasoning regarding Cynthia's new job. Sure, Cynthia has experience and actively campaigned for the position, but in Tracey's mind, they were equally qualified. She then reasons that Cynthia's race provided her with an unfair advantage in the competition for the position. Without including any meaningful evidence for this belief, Tracey's gossip intimates that Cynthia did not deserve the promotion and received the position for political reasons. Tracey's claims subtly reveal her true opinions about Black workers at Olstead. Tracey ultimately believes that although they may be good enough for physical labor, they are not suited for white-collar jobs involving analytics. The boldness with which she challenges Cynthia's suitability for the managerial position echoes racist tropes that rely on negative stereotypes about African-American people's intelligence.

Additionally, Tracey uses xenophobic ideological statements in her claims about the ease with which immigrants attain jobs in America. Throughout the play, Oscar is present in most scenes at the bar. The only character who openly interacts with him is Stan. Their working relationship guides their communication. However, the friendship group rarely communicates with Oscar. His invisibility to the patrons at Stan's bar emphasizes the challenges that immigrants face in successfully integrating into American society. Tracey's view of Oscar as a freeloading immigrant echoes White-nationalist, dog-whistle talking points regarding the supposed problems that immigrant workers create for native-born Americans. Ian Haney-Lopez explains that dog-whistle politics reference "coded racial appeals that carefully manipulate hostility toward nonwhites."[18] Tracey mimics racist dog whistles in her conversation with Oscar, which signals to the audience her perception about racial dynamics in the United States. Tracey's perception of Oscar is problematic, because she relies on racist and xenophobic tropes to justify her casual racism. She assumes that Oscar is an immigrant, despite his true identity. Oscar informs Tracey that he was born in America, but she dismisses this fact because it does not serve her narrow interpretation of the Latino citizens of Reading.

Tracey's argument lacks logic. Her claims present an undercurrent of racist ideologies in Reading. If the only people in positions of authority at the factory are White men, the promotion of a Black woman to the managerial rank would challenge the racial standards established at the company. She reasons that there are new racial politics at work that prevent some people from advancing while promoting other workers' success. Ironically, Tracey does not challenge the long-standing unwritten policies that prevent Black and Latino workers from gaining access to manufacturing jobs or managerial positions at

Olstead, because these policies previously benefited members of her racial community. It is only when diverse hires begin to shake up the company's dynamics that Tracey complains. Tracey claims that she is not prejudiced, but she is. Her racism manifests through her belief that White workers are better suited for managerial positions, and her xenophobia manifests through her arguments that native-born Americans belong in Olstead's manufacturing positions, whereas immigrants from Central America, South America, and the Caribbean are not entitled to these jobs.

Chris and Jason

The heart of the conflict between the workers at Olstead and the company bosses transitions into a fight between the strikers and their temporary replacements. In the grand scheme, the workers believed they had power, but the company called their bluff. Two generations of Olstead workers face conflict within their friend groups. Initially, the trio consisting of Jessie, Cynthia, and Tracey struggle to understand their place in a shifting economy, but they are not the only characters struggling to find a place in this new reality. Cynthia's son, Chris, and Tracey's son, Jason, both struggle to control their anger at their displacement from work. The shifts in time that Nottage uses throughout the play echo the connections between actions in 2000 and their lasting results in 2008. Starting with the strike, Chris and Jason make consequential choices that alter the trajectory of their lives. Ironically, instead of taking out their anger on company bosses, they fight with each other and project their frustrations on temporary workers at the plant who cross the picket line. Specifically, they attack Oscar. Through Oscar, Nottage characterizes how disenfranchised groups are manipulated by large companies during labor disputes. Instead of paying long-time workers a fair salary with benefits, companies like Olstead lock out workers and bring in a new batch of employees whom they can pay at a lower rate. This manipulative strategy cuts costs and breaks the illusion of community between workers and their place of employment. Another unfortunate consequence of this strategy is the contentious relationship that develops between the striking employees and the temporary workers. As the temporary workers literally cross the picket line, they put their lives at risk because the striking employees view them as "scabs" who have stolen their jobs. The conflict between both groups of employees demonstrates a need for more jobs and economic opportunity. A more effective strategy for addressing these issues might involve the creation of an alliance to yield fruitful results for both groups. However, the maneuvering of companies like Olstead ensures that neither group of workers empathizes with the other. Instead, they see each other as bitter rivals scrambling for the few opportunities presented.

The conflict in *Sweat* culminates in a physical altercation between Chris, Jason, Oscar, and Stan in act 2, scene 6. As Chris and Jason struggle to comprehend their next steps while the strike drags on, they view Oscar as an easy target to unleash their aggression. Their fight is egged on by a drunken Tracey, who belligerently continues to paint immigrant workers as thieves who have no business working at Olstead. After being hired at Olstead, Oscar quits his job at the bar in preparation for his new opportunity. When he comes to retrieve his belongings from work, the scene devolves into a melee, with neither side achieving much success. The conflict results in a devastating loss for Chris and Jason. During the fight, Jason is the clear aggressor, but Chris works with him to punish Oscar. An unintentional consequence of the fight occurs when, in a fit of rage, Jason grabs a bat from Stan's bar to attack Oscar and Stan. The aftermath of the fight is the frame that guides the drama of the play. Nottage uses dramatic shifts in time from 2000 to 2008 to show the audience the aftermath of the fight and what Chris and Jason lost in their battle. Chris and Jason both serve lengthy jail sentences and are released in 2008. Their freedom is tainted by the economic depression in 2008. If they Struggled to find employment in 2000, 2008 represents a worse situation. Their status as ex-convicts creates a significant barrier for their employment. Ironically, earlier in their lives, they benefited from the privilege of their respective familial legacy at Olstead. This was their key to landing a stable manufacturing job. After their time in jail, they are deemed outsiders and struggle to find minimum-wage positions.

The transition between Jason's and Chris's employment histories in *Sweat* begins in 2000 before the strike. Julie Burrell clarifies the central action in *Sweat* as "the effects of job loss on two generations of employees at a steel tubing plant, moving back and forth in time between 2000 and 2008, during which time the deindustrial revolution, exacerbated by the financial collapse of the post-9/11 era, has had devastating consequences on the lives of Nottage's characters."[19] As Olstead begins the difficult process of transitioning their plant to Mexico, workers in Reading struggle to understand their path forward. Both men consider the kind of lives they want to live. Jason seems content to follow the familial path carved out by years of dedicated service at Olstead, but Chris wants to chart a new course. He explains to Jason:

> Chris: I kinda wanna do something a little different than my moms and pops. Yo, I got aspirations. There it is. And I won't apologize.
> Jason: You got aspirations? What is this, Black History Month?
> Chris: As a matter of fact it is. You got a problem with that?
> Jason: If we're being perfectly honest, I get a little tired of the syrupy commercials. Actually, it shouldn't be called Black

> History Month, it should be called "Make White People Feel Guilty Month." Right, Stan?[20]

Jason is not supportive of Chris's ambitions. He projects his own fear onto Chris and uses racial microaggressions to emphasize his point. Through Jason, Nottage displays a rigidity of thought that is characteristic of White supremacists. Ironically, both Tracey and Jason have African-American friends. These friendships begin to unravel when Cynthia and Chris make choices to pursue their own ambitions. Chris wants to teach, whereas Jason believes that teaching is an undesirable profession. His claims reflect a narrow understanding of work. For Jason, his job satisfaction is evidenced primarily through his income. Chris asserts that job satisfaction can come from working in a purposeful position. Their conflict reveals fundamental differences in the way they view work. This conflict signals a possible fracture in their friendship. Ultimately, however, the fracture occurs not because of Chris's enrollment in college but through their brutal attack on Oscar and Stan.

The relationship between Chris and Jason devolves throughout the play. Both men signal different values. The problems they experience working at Olstead momentarily unites them through a collective battle against the temporary workers who cross the picket line, but their friendship was dissolving before their disastrous fight at Stan's bar. Once the men emerge from jail in 2008, they face new challenges in a depleted economic space. While in jail, Chris pursues his education and promises to finish his degree on the outside. On the other hand, Jason follows a different path, joining a White supremacist gang and getting provocative tattoos that announce his racist ideology to the world. The physical change exhibited through Jason's embrace of White supremacy demonstrates his desire to remain in control, despite his diminished standing in society. Simon Clark explains that

> there is little new in the ideas that underpin white nationalism, white supremacy, the alt-right, and fascism. At its core, white nationalism is little more than an attempt to cloak white supremacist ideas in the more respectable language of racial separatism, just as the alt-right has tried to repackage fascist thought in a more modern form. All these variants are built on common notions of a white identity and racial superiority. They promote hate and violence as valid political tools, rejecting values of equality, coexistence, and the rule of law in favor of raw power and ethnic division.[21]

In prison, Jason finds a new community. In jail, Jason joins a racist gang. Before he attacks Stan and Oscar, Jason's best friend was an African American. However, once in prison, Jason adopts extremist beliefs that initiated when immigrant workers crossed the picket line at Olstead. Jason enjoyed the benefits gained from working at Olstead and viewed the temporary workers (who were Latino) as interlopers. He shifts the blame from Olstead company managers to another, ultimately comparable, group of workers who are simply trying to establish a comfortable life. His views are fueled by hatred and misunderstanding. The consequence of his fight in 2000 manifests in a loss of all integrity which culminates in his struggle in 2008 to find his place in the world.

Conclusion

In act 2, scene 6, Stan asserts that "nostalgia's a disease. . . ."[22] His pronouncement poignantly challenges the perspectives held by Tracey and Jason. His ideas also challenge contemporary politicians who harness racial tensions to promote their own political agendas. For example, slogans like "Make America Great Again" harken back to an era when African Americans, Latinos, and other marginalized groups were denied opportunities in the United States. This coded language suggests that the past was a better time primarily for White men; yet, Nottage refrains from chastising racist characters in *Sweat*. Instead, she tries to unpack their beliefs to understand the source of their anger. In both cases, Tracey and Jason hold onto a deep-set fear regarding their place in the world. They fear being left behind as other workers enter the market. Instead of competing with their talents, they seek to rationalize the advancement of diverse workers in ways that dehumanize them. However, Tracey and Jason are not the only characters who struggle to reconcile their current position with their past. Jessie and Cynthia consider where they started at Olstead as young women with their current placement. Although they occupy different positions within the work environment, both understand that they sacrificed something for their continued employment. Whether their respective sacrifices were worth it is a question that guides their independent reflections. Michael Schulman notes that "each character in 'Sweat' commits a reprehensible act, whether it's Cynthia's failing to stand with her friends on the picket line or Tracey's exhibiting a newfound racism. The plays also give voice to marginalized lives."[23] In *Sweat*, Nottage explores economic problems in the United States by examining the lives of hard-working Americans. The characters in the play are human beings caught within a political game they are unable to win, because they rarely appreciate that the rules they cling to shift as employers seek to double profits and cut costs. The workers in *Sweat* believe that, through their dedication to Olstead they can achieve stability, but the fluctuating economic and political systems in which they live ensure that they achieve very little through their sacrifice.

CHAPTER 9

The Question of Values in *Mlima's Tale*

Directed by Jo Bonney, *Mlima's Tale* premiered on April 15, 2018, at the Public Theater in New York City. The play featured an ensemble cast including Sahr Ngaujah as Mlima and Ito Aghayere, Jojo Gonzalez, and Kevin Mambo portraying multiple characters throughout the play.[1] According to Nottage, *Mlima's Tale* was inspired by Kathryn Bigelow's 2014 animated documentary short titled *Last Days*, as well as Damon Tabor's article "The Ivory Highway," which was published in *Men's Journal* in the same year. Both texts paint a picture of the growing elephant poaching crisis in Africa. John Frederick Walker notes that "the 1989 CITES [Convention on International Trade in Endangered Species]-imposed ban didn't outlaw ivory, or address buying, selling, or possessing it. Within national borders. That's regulated by each country's law. The ban prohibits the international trade in raw and worked ivory, meaning tusks and carvings, with certain exceptions for antiques and sport-hunted trophies."[2] This law requires a global effort to enforce the ban on the international trade of ivory, but thus far, there has not been enough international cooperation to fully impede the poaching of elephants and importation of ivory.

According to Bigelow, "elephants in the wild could be extinct in 11 years."[3] Her film records the trajectory of elephant poaching by starting with the consumer. "When you buy something made of ivory, where does the money go?"[4] What follows is the path of the ivory backward, from product to animal. This visualization foregrounds the individual consumer's participation in a global enterprise that starts in Africa with the poaching of wild elephants and continues through transnational shipping organizations that span multiple countries and governments. *Last Days* is brief, but it paints a picture of how capitalism helps fund the extinction of a once large population of animals. While *Last*

Days paints a general picture of the problem of elephant poaching, "The Ivory Highway," more carefully describes the modern systems, including "sophisticated criminal syndicates—poachers, middlemen, traders, elusive kingpins—[that] increasingly dominate the trade."[5] Tabor's detailed article shows how poverty encourages individuals from economically developing countries to risk their lives to track elephants and trade in ivory. Both texts frame elephant poaching as a human-made problem connected to greed while focusing on the various forces required for the scheme to succeed.

Nottage extends the conversation by composing a didactic tale that teaches the audience about the horror of poaching from the perspective of an elephant lost to the trade: Mlima. Mlima is an elephant within the preserve and is known lovingly as "the mountain" because of his enormous size. Mlima is one of the largest elephants remaining in the preserve. *Mlima's Tale* explores the death of Mlima, a prized elephant murdered by poachers for his beautiful tusks. In his review of *Mlima's Tale*, Ben Brantley describes the play as a tale that follows the sale of "the tusks of the mighty Mlima, a legendary elephant struck down by poachers on the savannas of a Kenyan game preserve. Killing him entirely, it turns out, isn't possible. For wherever the ivory that once belonged to Mlima goes, so goes an entire baleful history of imperiled natural grandeur, leaving stains like marks of Cain on every one of its exploiters."[6] After Mlima is murdered, the actor portraying him metaphorically transforms into a ghost on stage while actors shift between disparate vignettes that explore the various figures involved in Mlima's murder and sale. On stage, Mlima is ever present, lurking as sellers and buyers haggle over the value of his ivory. The vignettes are connected by African proverbs. Before the action of a scene begins, a proverb is read aloud to the audience that connects to the specific conversation that follows. Instead of organizing the play in separate acts, Nottage chooses to include several scenes that shift seamlessly, stitched together by the lessons that the proverbs impart. Nottage uses this strategy to emphasize the connection between all players in the ivory trade. Within the play's running time of eighty minutes, Nottage weaves together the tragic tale of Mlima's life, death, and commodification.

By centering Mlima's perspective in the play, Nottage incorporates a critical perspective in the poaching discussion that is often lost. Nottage personifies Mlima and offers him an opportunity to teach the audience about his death while problematizing the economic forces at play. From the moment that Mlima is murdered, his ghost follows the path of his tusks from ivory sellers in Africa to the home of wealthy collectors in China. After Mlima's death, his spirit connects the various players of the animal trafficking scheme. While the human players consider the legality of poaching and the barriers to transporting Mlima's tusks, Mlima's spirit travels with his tusks and witnesses the routine transactions that accompany this brutal enterprise.

While teaching, Nottage avoids a self-righteous tone by emphasizing the routine nature of poaching. She reduces the grand scope of international animal trafficking by focusing on individuals within governmental and economic systems to demystify the processes that allow for Mlima's death. *Mlima's Tale* investigates the values present within market economies. Mlima represents the cost of exploiting Earth's gifts and the toll the plunder of natural resources has on human consciousness. Nottage explains "I see the play as being a distorted folktale, a cautionary tale. In African culture, there is a long tradition of teaching through folktales that have animals at the center."[7] By incorporating Mlima within the cast and dramatizing the materialistic ambitions of several human characters that result in the loss of Mlima's life, Nottage challenges the audience to consider the role they play in the exploitation of wildlife and their habitats.

Alma Jean Billingslea-Brown argues that African-American female writers have used folklore as a "a symbolic construction informed by ideology, tradition, and the artfulness of everyday life" that articulates "the values, beliefs, and ethos sustained and recreated in diaspora."[8] In *Mlima's Tale*, Nottage explores the consequences of poaching African elephants by tracing the steps of the economic system that profits from the elephants' deaths. Nottage uses Mlima as a character to narrate an individual story with global consequences. Mlima tells the story of his death and the commercialization of his tusks to teach the audience about the human values at odds with the survival of his species.

The Warning Within Mlima's Death

The story is organized into sixteen scenes. In scenes 1 and 16, a prologue and epilogue frame the narrative. In both scenes, Mlima recounts the years of his life and gives a warning to his family.

> Milma (*shouting*): If you're listening, remember, I count forty-eight from memory, five summers of died grass. Mumbi, if you hear me, don't come to mourn me. Run! Run! RUN![9]

Nottage personifies Mlima by situating the elephant within a familial structure. As his death approaches, Mlima recalls the stories that older elephants have told him. He begins with his grandmother remembering how she cautioned him to "listen to the night . . . listen with your entire body, feel how the earth shifts when there's the slightest disruption. . . ."[10] One of Mlima's earliest memories flashes before he succumbs to the hunters' weapons. The memory represents the first lesson the playwright seeks to teach her audience. Through Mlima, Nottage encourages her audience to pay attention to the changes in nature and consider how these changes have an impact on an individual's life. What responsibility do everyday people have for large-scale shifts in the environment? These questions offer the audience an opportunity to consider their individual or communal involvement in global environmental issues by seeing the consequences of poaching on Mlima and his family.

The revelation of Mlima's lessons continues as he realizes that early stories from youth were warnings of the danger he would encounter as an adult. Mlima remembers his mother and childhood friends. Nottage incorporates elements of African and African-American folklore within the play. In African-American literature, folktales are used to reflect cultural values and teach important lessons. Nottage utilizes this traditional form to create a narrative that exposes a global problem to her audience. This strategy is didactic in nature. Her lessons regarding the global ivory trade explore a problem that many might feel does not impact them. However, Nottage utilizes the issue of animal poaching to offer an ecocritical critique on the relationship between humans and nature. By centralizing Mlima's plight, Nottage demonstrates how people's consumption of environmental resources stresses our ecosystem and alters the composition of our civilization.

Scene 1 begins with a gruesomeness that sets the stage for her audience to consider the significance of Mlima's life literally and symbolically. The initial stage directions describe the scene as "a wilderness where a big tusker might seek refuge. The savannah. Full moon. Mlima, an elephant sensing danger, calls out to his fellow travelers."[11] Mlima speaks to characters who are not present. He calls out to his wife, children, and friends. He remembers his elders and past family members who passed down lessons to him that were meant to teach strategies for survival in a dangerous environment. As the audience witnesses Mlima's death, he remembers a lesson once given by his grandmother: "How you listen can mean the difference between life and death."[12] This statement is delivered to the audience, signaling the drama that will unfold. Nottage encourages the audience to listen to Mlima's life lessons to understand the context that creates a market for his death. Literally, Mlima is stalked by poor Somali hunters who have been tasked with retrieving eight tusks for their boss. However, they seek out Mlima specifically. Mlima is a great elephant with huge tusks worth much more than eight typical tusks. The decision to kill Mlima shows the audience an example of how materialism can influence one's behavior. The hunters have specific instructions, but their greed overrides those directives.

Traditionally, elephants symbolize wealth. They also symbolize memory. Nottage relies on the connection between memory and elephants by incorporating Mlima's memories into the narrative. However, she also foregrounds the hunter's memories. For the hunters, Mlima represents economic opportunity—his treasured tusks represent the culmination of several weeks of work—yet this hunt is also an opportunity to demonstrate their masculinity. One hunter named Geedi recalls a lesson his father taught him. "He tell me there be no sport in killing elephant, unless you kill with bow and arrow spear, like warrior. It is a creature to be respected, you must look it in the eye as it die. Give it the honor of knowing the hand that sent him to the other side."[13] Geedi's personal familial history reveals his ideas about manhood. For Geedi, a real hunter does not shoot with a gun. Instead, he uses his ability to demonstrate his mastery of the craft. In this moment, Mlima's death shows the audience how Geedi's view of self is connected to the life and death of Mlima. For Geedi, Mlima's death confirms his professionalism and masculinity simultaneously, because he has used his prowess to defeat a great foe. Mlima's reputation as the mountain provides Geedi with a sense of dignity despite the brutality of his actions. [14] In scene 2, as Mlima dies, Geedi reflects on the hunt as an extension of the values he was taught by his father. Geedi views Mlima as a worthy opponent whose death symbolizes his superior skill. Thus, the value of Mlima's life is viewed as an opportunity for a man to demonstrate his superiority through his physical conquest of an elephant.

Consequences for Mlima's Death

Nottage begins *Mlima's Tale* with the death of an elephant. His seemingly insignificant death becomes a catalyst to examine the connection between commodities and ecological plunder. The narrative begins in the African savannah, but the journey of the tusks is global. Beginning in a Kenyan bush and ending in a penthouse apartment in a Chinese high rise, Nottage exposes the journey that the tusks undergo, a journey that dramatizes human greed through the lens of the ivory trade. After Mlima's death, Nottage takes the audience on a journey with the tusks, from elephant to trinket. By leading the audience on this journey, Nottage minimizes the value of the product at the end of the trade by questioning the audience's attachment to goods. Nottage interrogates the value of the goods created from Mlima's tusks by exposing the illegal trade of ivory. She foregrounds Mlima's spirit, which destabilizes the worth of the finished products displayed at the end of the play.

After Mlima's death, the play explores Mlima's journey from elephant to artifact. The organization of the play shows how different characters' respective desires for money upends the legal barriers put in place to prevent the sale of ivory. Starting in Kenya, the audience is introduced to a series of officials who are responsible for protecting elephants and other national treasures. However, each character has an individual agenda that challenges their obligations. The characters frequently falter by choosing an outcome that emphasizes personal benefits. Nottage demystifies the elephant poaching crisis by centering encounters between individuals. From local lawmakers to artisans, the meetings between various characters emphasize competing personal agendas that fluctuate depending on what the parties value. One might value reputation, whereas the other values money. In either circumstance, the audience becomes privy to private conversations that demonstrate how communal values fluctuate when an opportunity for success is presented.

Present within each encounter is the actor portraying Mlima. Mlima is reduced throughout the play. Initially presented as a strong elephant, he is figuratively dismembered on stage, and his tusks are transported from the elephant preserve to various global sites. The ghost of Mlima observes the encounters between the principal players in the ivory trade. As each person succumbs to their own desires, Mlima marks them with a white residue. This residue symbolizes the consequences of their desires. Nottage continually questions what is valued through these minute encounters. Although Mlima's death features prominently, each participant within the trade exchanges their integrity for a present desire. Through these exchanges, Nottage continually asks the question "What do we value?"

In scenes 4 and 5, problems arise, as figureheads within the Kenyan government face questions about the consequences of Mlima's death. One key question that permeates the entire text is "How could this happen?" Scene 4 responds to this question directly when Githinji, a local police chief, quarrels with his nephew, Wamwara, a warden of the elephant sanctuary, about the role local leaders play in the continuation of the ivory trade. Several explanations for the continuation of the trade are given, including low wages for locals, the negative effect that elephants have on local farms, and the lack of manpower to keep track of the far-roaming animals. Any one of these issues could result in problems with elephant herds, but they do not explain the continued market for ivory goods or the willingness of local officials to turn a blind eye to the problem.

(Githinji casually reaches into his desk and passes Wamwara an envelope across the table.)
Githinji: That may help.
Wamwara: Is that what you think I'm here for?
Githinji: . . .

Wamwara: No. Not this time.

Githinji: C'mon. Don't thank me. It's a gift from your favorite Uncle. That's all.[15]

This conversation suggests a pattern of behavior of exchanging money to overlook poaching. The personal and professional relationships between the characters complicate their work obligations. Wamwara's relationship with his uncle is strained. He wants to find the culprit but is also motivated by money. In the past, he has taken resources from his uncle and turned a blind eye to Githinji's involvement in poaching. Now Wamwara unsuccessfully seeks to establish boundaries with his uncle. He cannot reset their relationship and assert new boundaries once Mlima has been killed, because the customs established with Githinji privilege money over policies to protect the wildlife in the preserve.

Githinji is not the only local official focused more on himself than his job. Andrew, the director of wildlife at the national park, shifts focus from Mlima to himself as well. Wamwara reports to Andrew and demands answers from him about Mlima's death. Andrew is responsible for accounting for the problems the preserve is facing. The goal of his response is to reassure his audience, including the media, that the culprits responsible for Mlima's death have been captured. His performance of justice undermines his role as director. For Andrew, presenting a culprit is more important than finding the responsible criminals.

Andrew: Yes. Yes. Yes. Fine. But all I want to know is, could these be our culprits?

Wamwara: . . . No. Amateurs. But it is something.

Andrew: (*impatient*) I don't think you understood what I was asking. I need more than conjecture. So, I'm going to ask you again, are these the poachers that killed Mlima?! (*A moment. Wamwara contemplates the question. Mlima appears, an imposing presence.*)

Wamwara: . . . Yes.[16]

The pressure to account for the death of Mlima encourages Wamwara to lie. He wants to capture the culprits, but he faces limitations from his administrators and local police force. His desire to hold the responsible poachers accountable for their actions is superseded by his desire to please his boss. As a result, the conflict between his boss and the media supersedes Wamwara's obligation to the animal preserve.

The media uproar surrounding Mlima's death matters more to Andrew than creating meaningful solutions to prevent poaching. Moreover, the international attention encourages local officials to present a scapegoat for Mlima's death. The individuals blamed for Mlima's death are poachers, but they are not the individuals responsible for this act. Punishing them creates a false sense of justice and does nothing to address the critical infrastructure problems that allow elephant deaths in Kenya. Nottage dramatizes the inability of local officials to create change by demonstrating their competing interests. These three men have responsibilities to fulfill their obligations to the community they serve, but no one holds them accountable. The lack of accountability allows different forces that govern each man's moral compass to direct their path forward. For Githinji, his role as local police chief affords him an opportunity to utilize his position to enrich himself. Wamwara's despair at his inability to provide results makes him susceptible to corruption. His lack of resources inspires his willingness to agree with Andrew's plan. Andrew's position requires him to present a strong response to the crimes committed at his park. He is focused on how he and the park are viewed instead of addressing the problems directly. Nottage uses the internal and external conflicts within and between the three local Kenyan officials to dramatize challenges facing antipoaching forces. Without a unified coalition working to protect natural resources, individual agendas will supplant their collective goal to protect the elephants.

Mlima's Journey Abroad

Although Mlima's tusks are extremely valuable, they also expose those found with them to legal action. In scene 7, Hassan Abdulla, a local businessman, seeks to discharge them quickly at a party at the local Chinese embassy. Hassan tempts Guoxi, a Chinese reporter, with the tusks, hoping to strike a deal that would benefit both parties. Although Guoxi behaves as though he was shocked by the possibility of an exchange, he acknowledges that ivory goods connect to his family's heritage. Guoxi describes an old familial heirloom. "My grandfather managed to hold on to a beautiful ivory caving of Quan Yin, the goddess of compassion. . . . It was so . . . intricate, lovely. It felt like a rare blessing that had been bestowed on our family."[17] Guoxi remembers the beauty of the statue and associates this memory with joy. Additionally, Guoxi reveals that "it was destroyed during a fire," and he secretly desires to replace the figurine.[18] Guoxi's memories emphasize an emotional feeling associated with the ivory statue of his past. The value of the lost figurine connects to a past that Guoxi treasures and seeks to replicate in the present. However, in the present, there are consequences for trading ivory that complicate his efforts to acquire a similar treasure. The rules that are put in place to protect Mlima and others like him are symbolic. These laws promote new values that appreciate the importance of natural resources. However, the ability of officials to undermine new laws demonstrates the fragility of regulations to protect animals like Mlima. The play shows how our values are emphasized by the individual choices made to facilitate deeply held desires. Mlima's life diminishes in worth when the opportunity for profits emerges.

In scene 7, Nottage dramatizes the danger surrounding Mlima's tusks departure from Africa. Mlima's departure from Kenya is fraught with complex transactions between shippers and legal officers. Every character along the way is aware of the unlawfulness of the ivory trade, yet they manage to manipulate regulations to achieve a desired result. Greed guides the transport of Mlima's tusks throughout the play, driving key players to take larger risks to gain quick financial results. One group of handlers reconsiders the plan to ship Mlima's tusks from the port of Mombasa.

> Hassan Abdulla: What do you think?
> Aziz Muhammad: I don't like it. Not now. Timing feels bad.
> Hassan Abdulla: Why?
> Aziz Muhammad: Heat is everywhere. It's dangerous in Mombasa. MLIMA is in the news every day. They are watching us.
> Hassan Abdulla: I have a promising buyer. Someone well placed and a powerful ally, here and abroad.[19]

After Hassan makes a contact with Guoxi, he quickly moves to transport Mlima's tusks. His eagerness troubles local handler Aziz, who has already established a clear plan for the movement of Mlima's tusks, but with the guarantee of money and a new relationship with a member of the Chinese embassy, Hassan considers this transaction as a bridge to more economic endeavors. Hassan is blinded by the opportunity and readily risks his enterprise to ensure that the tusks are secured and moved out of Kenya quickly for the benefit of his new associate. His behavior undermines new local regulations and jeopardizes the entire shipment, but he is willing to take the risk if he can ensure a profit.

Mlima's death echoes throughout the local press with additional attention focused on nearby ports. The tension between lawmakers and shippers is most pronounced with Captain Ramaaker, an American captain who is committed to "running clean."[20] In the past, he has willingly shipped contraband in his cargo. However, Mlima's tusks are politicized, and he does not want to risk jail time or slowing down the transit of legally acquired goods on his ships. Although Ramaaker rebuffs Aziz Muhammad, Aziz is able to transport Mlima's tusks on the ship. In scene 9, Aziz bribes the chief mate, Jim Baxter, with three-and-a-half percent worth the cost of the tusks to sneak the prized tusks onto the ship. Baxter utilizes his position as chief mate to make a quick deal that jeopardizes the entire shipment. This slip in integrity undermines his relationship with his captain, but the opportunity to earn money entices him.

Ramaaker fears criminal responsibility for the discovery of Mlima's tusks on his ship. He is aware that he will be held responsible if any materials that are not listed on the ship's manifest are found on the boat by local officials. In Hao Phong, Vietnam, Ramaaker's fears are realized when the contraband is found. However, local officials are not interested in punishing him. Instead, they seek to claim the goods for themselves to make a profit. To avoid responsibility for the contraband, Ramaaker states, "the container is not mine, and therefore I take no responsibility for its contents. If things were to go missing, I couldn't vouch for them."[21] He is allowed to continue with his work as the tusks move closer to their final destination in China. Nottage's characterization of the shipping process again emphasizes the corruption of local officials who value economic gain over the preservation of life. Without fail, the new regulations established to diminish the ivory trade fail to achieve their goal. Mlima's presence alongside the port workers frames the true cost of the exchange.

Nottage emphasizes that the poaching industry has devastated the population of elephants in Africa. Mlima is present during each transaction though he remains silent. However, in scene 10, Mlima's voice and other voices echo through the boughs of the boat. The stage directions characterize the sounds as "elephant memories."[22] Notably, Nottage lists the voices named and indicates their relationship to other elephants. For example, "Kade, son of Gatimu . . . Nyawira, sister of Kacey."[23] The personification of elephant lives witnessed through the citing of relationships creates a gloomy mood that channels a litany of lost souls. Nottage presents elephants as members of larger families to stress their collective importance. Her goal is to present the ivory trade as more than an economic enterprise. By visualizing the trade as an attack on individuals that are part of families, Nottage challenges the audience to consider the impact of the trade on kinship bonds.

How does the loss of a brother, mother, or sister change the depiction of poaching from an attack on animals into an act that destroys families? Elizabeth A. Archie et al. claim that "elephants—both Asian and African—live in . . . social groups (also called families, family units, or family cores)."[24] Nottage's emphasis on familial structures within the elephant community urges the audience to consider the connection between the social lives of elephants and humans. Instead of envisioning the animals as separate from our lives, she promotes a different perspective to combat the separation that people might feel from the problem. Hearing the voices of the animals lost to the ivory trade suggests that the ivory trade is immoral because of the destruction of family units. Notably, this scene contrasts previous scenes that focus exclusively on human participants in the trade that unscrupulously pursue money with lost family members begging to be remembered. In this way, Nottage personifies elephants by focusing on their kinship and challenges the audience to find the humanity in the human characters who value money instead of life.

Next, the ivory trade flows into artisanal workshops globally, where the ivory is transformed into highly stylized treasures. The handiwork associated with the sculptures reflects a cultural heritage that extends to previous generations. Earlier in the play, Guoxi reminisces about the honor associated with possessing a carefully crafted ivory carving within his family. With new laws, the ability to continue this specific handicraft tradition has diminished because of the inability to legally obtain source material. However, the market has not collapsed, because smugglers that work alongside artisans find innovative strategies to source ivory. Nevertheless, there is danger connected to this field. In scene 13, Nottage dramatizes the negotiations between artisan Master Yee and ivory dealer Thuy Fan to emphasize the questionable nature of the continued work.

> Master Yee: Is there anything that I need to know before I begin?
> Thuy Fan: Why? Is there something wrong?
> Master Yee: I'm cautious these days, the ban has made it hard to focus on my craft. Suddenly, I feel like a criminal for doing what I have always done.
> Thuy Fan: The officials don't know any better. I wouldn't worry.
> Master Yee: I'm a Buddhist. I could not conscience killing for my craft. All of our pieces in the workshop, their provenance is clean, from older stockpiles. I need your assurance that this was procured in a legal and ethical manner.
> Thuy Fan: Yes, yes.[25]

Master Yee questions the authenticity of the material but demands no records to ensure that the tusks were obtained in a lawful manner. This interaction dramatizes how the new regulations regarding ivory poaching have complicated the craft. However, from its inception people have worked around the rules to continue the ivory trade. Every party within the trade is culpable for the continued massacre of elephants for their tusks.

Scene 14 represents the culmination of Mlima's journey from vital father, son, and husband to sculpture. The tragedy of his death is accentuated through the environment of the upscale ivory shop. The shop displays carved tusks in the shapes of various trinkets for sale. The mood of the scene is overwhelmingly shallow. Alice Ying is described as "nouveau riche, talks loudly into a Bluetooth device for her cell phone, absently, perusing the shop" while "Mr. Cheung, an obsequious salesman, trails closely behind her."[26] Nottage presents the final transaction between Alice and Mr. Cheung differently than the communications between the past dealers on the ivory trade. This part of the trade seems less encumbered than the interactions that occurred in Kenya, largely because ivory is connected to a long tradition of artistry in China. Nevertheless, the optics of the trade are considered in the sales transaction as Cheung tempts Alice with various goods. "What you see is mostly older ivory from before the ban. (*lowers his voice*) But, if it is new ivory, then it must be from a dead elephant, or the tusks fall out when they get old, but they always grow back like teeth. So needn't worry, our certificates are in order."[27] Mr. Cheung misrepresents the origins of the art in his shop. However, it is unclear whether he is knowledgeable regarding the brutality that elephants face when their tusks are harvested. What is clear is that he is focused most on the sale. To alleviate any perceived moral hesitation of the buyer, Cheung makes an untrue physiological assertion regarding regrowing tusks. The certificates that report the origins of the tusks are as reliable as the regulations put in place to dampen the ivory trade. They are hollow symbols that do not protect elephants. Instead, the certificates are meant to make people feel better about their actions.

Ultimately, the sale is completed, and Mlima's tusk, represented through the actor's regal pose, is exchanged for money. Although Alice stands in awe of the beauty of the art piece, she does not understand the significance of the life represented in the art. Alice is shopping for a statement piece for her new apartment. According to Mr. Cheung, the sculpture is worth 7.4 million yuan or roughly 1.42 million dollars. The artwork represents a demonstration of wealth for the young shopper. Her purchase suggests her status; meanwhile the voices of other elephants can be heard in this scene. The audience hears them, but the salesman and customer do not. The voices of the elephants are meant for the ears of the audience alone. These voices restate the elephants' role within the families they have left behind. The beauty of the shop takes on an ugly glare when considered through the lens of these memories. These final moments of the play encourage the audience to consider values. Why should the reputation of Alice within her social group matter more than the lives of elephants in Kenya? Nottage poses questions that encourage introspection and, hopefully, change.

Mlima's Remains

Mlima's death and subsequent transformation into a statue displayed in a nouveau riche Chinese home portrays the continued issue of the ivory trade. Nottage dramatizes this global problem by personifying Mlima and exposing the various people responsible for his death. By examining each step of the trade from poachers to collectors, Nottage highlights the various players that benefit from the murder of elephants. The problem of elephant poaching is complicated by each person's participation, yet everyone's participation can be linked to their individual interests. The respective goals of the participants overshadow the death tolls that outnumber the birth rates of African elephants. The expansive enterprise will continue unless a global coalition emerges to collectively address the issue. Until that point, Mlima's death and journey will continue for countless other elephants, likely resulting in the extinction of that population.

Conclusion

The Future Is Nottage and Elusive Justice in *Clyde's*

Lynn Nottage's oeuvre includes several plays, musicals, and television work, but she is best known as the only female playwright to win two Pulitzer Prizes for her theatrical productions. Her status as a critical success is complimented by the widespread public appeal of her plays. Some playwrights enjoy critical success or public acclaim, but Nottage is the rare figure who has achieved praise in both arenas. Her latest Broadway success, *Clyde's*, has further cemented Nottage's staying power, nearly three decades after she began her professional career.

Clyde's debuted on Broadway at the Helen Hayes Theater in November 2021 and closed in January 2022. It was directed by Kate Whoriskey and included an ensemble cast that featured Kara Young, Ron Cephas Jones, Uzo Aduba, Reza Salazar, and Edmund Donovan. *New York Times* writer Michael Paulson noted that, in 2022, "an annual survey by American Theater magazine . . . found that Nottage's sandwich shop comedy, 'Clyde's,' will be the most-produced play in the country this season, with at least 11 productions. The survey also found that there were 24 productions of Nottage plays planned [that] season, which ties her with the perennial regional theater favorite Lauren Gunderson for the title of most produced playwright in America."[1]

Originally titled *Floyd's*, that version of the play ran from July 27 to August 31, 2019, at Minneapolis's Guthrie Theater, which commissioned the work. This earlier version of the play included a truck stop owner named Floyd. This character was eliminated from the final version. Karen Bovard of

Broadway World described Floyd (portrayed by Johanna Day) as "a real mean woman who 'doesn't do pity' but chooses to employ ex-incarcerated people."[2] In *Clyde's*, Nottage continues her commitment to social criticism by infusing the play with a political candor tempered by humor. The ingredients of a typical Lynn Nottage production are present, including a multicultural cast addressing political issues in a pragmatic way. In many ways, *Clyde's* represents a continuation of her earlier Pulitzer Prize-winning work *Sweat*, set in Reading, Pennsylvania. However, where *Sweat* examined marginalized factory workers facing the reality of their jobs being shipped overseas, *Clyde's* focuses on a different group of workers altogether: people formerly incarcerated. Michelle Alexander explains, "a criminal record today authorizes precisely the forms of discrimination we supposedly left behind—discrimination in employment, housing, education, public benefits, and jury service. Those labeled criminals can even be denied the right to vote."[3] This cast of characters is very different from the characters in *Sweat*. In *Sweat*, we see a group of dedicated blue-collar workers lose their jobs during an economic collapse and the fallout that ensues. However, *Clyde's* focuses on a group of outcasts struggling to find work because of their status as ex-convicts. The cooks at *Clyde's* each represent the real-life issues that place people squarely within the American carceral system.

Set in an average truck stop outside Reading, Pennsylvania, *Clyde's* is run by the gruff and mysterious manager Clyde, an African-American woman who takes pleasure in tormenting her kitchen staff, Montrellous, Letitia, Rafael, and Jason. Each cook has their own story that details their specific fall resulting in time spent in jail; their personal narratives reflect national issues such as the cost of prescription medication and drug addiction. Each character in *Clyde's* makes their way to the restaurant as a last-ditch effort to remain out of jail. Many of them have tried to obtain jobs in other industries. However, their respective past lives impede their growth in the present. Clyde takes in these wayward individuals and instead of providing them with opportunities, she relishes demeaning them. The workers are thus kept in a state of limbo, where they want to progress, but the routes forward are blocked to them.

Clyde's combines myth with reality as the setting shifts from the drudgery of everyday life to the possibilities of the fantastic. Each crew member fantasizes about crafting the perfect sandwich. On the surface, their desires do not make sense. Faced with the reality of falling back into criminal patterns that keep many people in an endless cycle of incarceration, the characters spend their time at work considering recipes for successful dishes. The perfect sandwich represents an extended metaphor for finding a solution for their individual issues. While Letitia dreams of the perfect sauce and Jason practices applying the best garnish to a sandwich, their focus on food reflects a fixation on controlling what little they can in their situations. In their minds, who they are is not defined by the mistakes they have made or jail sentences. The ingredients for the perfect sandwich embody a willingness to work to self-correct past mistakes in hopes of taking a different path.

In *Clyde's*, Nottage anticipates future social problems. Although the truck stop diner would have been an innocuous setting when the play was first performed in 2019, it resounded with new meaning in 2021 as the world battled an ever-present pandemic that ground the economy to a stop. Globally, nations struggled with bottleneck shipping catastrophes that impacted the transmission of goods from one part of the world to the other. Food shortages that resulted in near riots at local grocery stores transformed overnight who was deemed an essential worker. In the past, a restaurant cook or busboy might not have garnered respect. However, under the glaring light of food and labor shortages, the food that we eat and those who prepare it shifted from the margins to the center of conversations about livable wages. In this political climate, the truck stop was the perfect place for a conversation about the problems that everyday people face. The stage directions describe the setting as a

> Truck stop sandwich shop, it sits on a nondescript stretch of road, in Berks County, Pennsylvania, traveled by those looking for shortcuts, detours or merely escape. It is a strange liminal space populated by folx down on their luck and looking for a second chance at life. Frequented by truckers and the occasional local, Clyde's like many small businesses in post-industrial America, is trying hard to survive and carve out space in a rapidly evolving landscape. We are in the kitchen, but it could be limbo.[4]

Nottage plays with elements of the surreal in *Clyde's*. Although grounded in a real-world setting, the play poses big questions about how society addresses social problems. When interviewed about *Clyde's*, Nottage mused "*Clyde's* is a play about people trapped in a liminal space. It is also about community, healing, creativity, mindfulness and forgiveness."[5] For Nottage, the heart of the play focuses on people who want to move forward but are struggling. Her specific focus on a community that is underexamined in theatre reflects her commitment to centering marginalized people's narratives on the stage. The cooks' humanity shines through as they struggle to move on after paying their debts to society.

Nottage replicates the consequences of prison life on stage by forcing the audience to witness the lived experience of individuals who are often considered unredeemable. The audience only sees the characters in the kitchen of the truck stop restaurant, and the kitchen replicates the prison, as the cooks are worked hard with few rewards by a merciless manager who resembles a sadistic prison guard. Angela Davis posits that "prison therefore functions ideologically as an abstract site into which undesirables are deposited, relieving us of the responsibility of thinking about the real issues afflicting those communities from which prisoners are drawn in such disproportionate numbers. This is the ideological work that the prison performs."[6] Nottage unravels the work of the prison by presenting people on the stage who struggle to maintain an average existence. She privileges their humanity by not foregrounding their problems; instead, she showcases the simplicity of their desires despite the tragedy of their circumstances. Ultimately, Nottage crafts a play about people who were prisoners and are now imprisoned by social systems that limit their possibilities. Despite these limitations, the characters remain hopeful by coming into the truck stop and going to work. Their collective goal of staying outside of the system drives their compliance with their tyrannical boss in scenes that juxtapose comedy with suspense.

Clyde's represents the future for Nottage's works while maintaining a commitment to her original political agenda. Nottage's plays frequently consider the narratives of marginalized figures. In this play, she utilizes the characters as symbolic of social problems that plague society. Her commitment to social criticism links her to African-American female playwrights from far and recent past including Angelina Weld Grimké, Alice Childress, Ntozake Shange, and contemporary playwrights such as Suzan-Lori Parks. Moreover, *Clyde's* represents an extension of her initial goal to create dynamic narratives about multicultural communities with Black women at the center of discourse. Her initial works such as *Crumbs from the Table of Joy*, *Intimate Apparel*, and *Fabulation* situated African-American women in the center of these communities, thereby shining a light on their largely untold stories. However, in this text, Nottage creates a text with an African-American woman as the villain. In *Clyde's*, Nottage affords her Black female manager a position of power within the truck stop sandwich shop. Nottage departs from the pattern used by past writers who addressed respectability politics by encouraging her audience to recognize the full complexity of Black women without requiring that Black heroines be moral.

NOTES

Chapter 1: An Introduction to Lynn Nottage

1. "Lynn Nottage to Students: Replace Judgment with Curiosity."
2. Brown, "Lynn Nottage's Sweat and Blood."
3. Schulman, "The First Theatrical Landmark of the Trump Era."
4. Schulman, "The First Theatrical Landmark of the Trump Era."
5. Stratton, "In Conversation: Lynn Nottage & Paula Vogel," 15.
6. Gener, "Conjurer of Worlds," 23.
7. Shannon, "An Interview with Lynn Nottage," 195.
8. Shannon, "An Interview with Lynn Nottage," 195.
9. Nottage, *POOF!* 96.
10. Catanese, Brandi Wilkins. "Taking the Long View." 550.
11. Shannon, "An Intimate Look at the Plays of Lynn Nottage," 188.
12. Maxwell, "Lynn Nottage: There Are Not Many People Who Look Like Me Who Have Been Writing Plays for 25 Years."

Chapter 2: Migration in *Crumbs from the Table of Joy*

1. Harris, *The Great Migration North, 1910–1970.*
2. Nottage, *Crumbs*, 8.
3. Nottage, *Crumbs*, 14.
4. Nottage, *Crumbs*, 10.
5. Wilkerson, *The Warmth of Other Suns*, 9.
6. Griffith, *Who Set You Flowin? The African-American Migration Narrative*, 4.
7. Berlin, *The Making of African America: The Four Great Migrations*, 155.
8. Rodgers, *Canaan Bound: The African American Migration Novel*, 4.
9. Rothstein, "Round Five for a Theatrical Heavyweight," *New York Times*, April 15, 1990. https://www.nytimes.com/1990/04/15/theater/.
10. Shannon, "A Transplant That Did Not Take: August Wilson's Views on the Great Migration." *African American Review* 31, no. 4 (1997): 660. https://doi.org/10.2307/3042334.
11. Nottage, *Crumbs*, 11.
12. Stars, "When God Drove a Cadillac: The Remarkable Story of Father Divine."
13. Nottage, *Crumbs*, 12.
14. Nottage, *Crumbs*, 19–20.

15. Watts, *God, Harlem USA: The Father Divine Story*, x.
16. Watts, *God, Harlem USA: The Father Divine Story*, x.
17. Watts, *God, Harlem USA: The Father Divine Story*, x.
18. Nottage, *Crumbs*, 28.
19. Nottage, *Crumbs*, 28.
20. Burnham, *God Comes to America: Father Divine and the Peace Mission Movement*, 48.
21. Nottage, *Crumbs*, 73.
22. Jones, "An End to the Neglect of the Problems of the Negro Woman! (1949)."
23. Nottage, *Crumbs*, 82.
24. Hutchinson, *Blacks and Reds: Race and Class in Conflict* (East Lansing: Michigan State University Press, 1995), 109.
25. Nottage, *Crumbs*, 34.
26. Nottage, *Crumbs*, 36.
27. Solomon, *The Cry Was Unity: Communists and African Americans 1917–1936*, 22.
28. Kelley, *Freedom Dreams: The Black Radical Imagination*, 136.
29. Nottage, *Crumbs*, 80.
30. Nottage, *Crumbs*, 82.
31. Hall, "The Long Civil Rights Movement and the Political Uses of the Past."
32. Nottage, *Crumbs*, 17.
33. Nottage, *Crumbs*, 76–77
34. Nottage, *Crumbs*, 78.
35. Nottage, *Crumbs*, 58.
36. Nottage, *Crumbs*, 88.

Chapter 3: Humanizing Terror on the Stage in *Por'Knockers* and *Mud, River, Stone*

1. Sommer, Elyse. "A *CurtainUp* Review: *Mud, River, Stone.*"
2. Dickson-Carr, *African American Satire: The Sacredly Profane Novel*, 18.
3. "Political Theatre," 17.
4. Nottage, *Por'Knockers*, 118.
5. Nottage, *Por'Knockers*, 119.
6. Nottage, *Por'Knockers*, 119.
7. Nottage, *Por'Knockers*, 119.
8. Nottage, *Por'Knockers*, 120.
9. Ranstorp, "Terrorism in the Name of Religion," 43–44.
10. Nottage, *Por'Knockers*, 123.
11. Juergensmeyer, *Terror in the Mind of God: The Global Rise of Religious Violence*, 122.
12. Wallace, *Black Macho and the Myth of the Superwoman*, 7.
13. Nottage, *Por'Knockers*, 139.
14. Nottage, *Por'Knockers*, 143.
15. Nottage, *Mud, River, Stone*, 164.
16. Fanon, *The Wretched of the Earth*, 2.

17. Nottage, *Mud, River, Stone*, 170.
18. Nottage, *Mud, River, Stone*, 170.
19. Nottage, *Mud, River, Stone*, 184–85.
20. Press, *Rogue Empires: Contracts and Conmen in Europe's Scramble for Africa*, 166.
21. Nottage, *Mud, River, Stone*, 186.
22. Nottage, *Mud, River, Stone*, 168.
23. Nottage, *Mud, River, Stone*, 168.
24. Nottage, *Mud, River, Stone*, 188.
25. Nottage, *Mud, River, Stone*, 188.
26. Nottage, *Mud, River, Stone*, 216.
27. Press, *Rogue Empires: Contracts and Conmen in Europe's Scramble for Africa*, 166.
28. Nottage, *Mud, River, Stone*, 210.
29. Fanon, *The Wretched of the Earth*, 93–94.
30. Nottage, *Mud, River, Stone*, 241.
31. Nottage, *Mud, River, Stone*, 241.
32. Nottage, *Mud, River, Stone*, 242.

Chapter 4: Reclaiming a Voice from the Past in *Las Meninas*

1. CUNYTV, "Women in Theatre: Lynn Nottage."
2. Walker, *In Search of Our Mothers' Gardens*, 87.
3. Nottage, *Las Meninas*, 251–52.
4. Nottage, *Las Meninas*, 324.
5. Nottage, *Las Meninas*, 248.
6. Fraser, *Love and Louis XIV: The Women in the Life of the Sun King*, 103.
7. Levi, *Louis XIV*, 151.
8. Foucault, *The Order of Things*, 16.
9. Foucault, *The Order of Things*, 16.
10. Berger, *The Success and Failure of Picasso*, 185.
11. Miles, "If It's Baroque, Don't Fix It," 173.
12. Nottage, *Las Meninas*, 252.
13. Stockho, "French Paintings of the Seventeenth and Eighteenth Centuries," 3.
14. Nottage, *Las Meninas*, 254–55.
15. Nottage, *Las Meninas*, 256.
16. Nottage, *Las Meninas*, 263–64.
17. Kamen, *Empire: How Spain Became a World Power*, 411.
18. Kamen, *Empire: How Spain Became a World Power*, 56.
19. Kamen, *Empire: How Spain Became a World Power*, 57.
20. Nottage, *Las Meninas*, 284.
21. Nottage, *Las Meninas*, 285.
22. Nottage, *Las Meninas*, 286.
23. De Montespan, *Memoirs of Madame La Marquise De Montespan*, chap. XL.
24. Nottage, *Las Meninas*, 237.
25. Nottage, *Las Meninas*, 304.

26. Nottage, *Las Meninas*, 305.
27. Nottage, *Las Meninas*, 306.
28. Nottage, *Las Meninas*, 306.

Chapter 5: Marriage and Respectability in *Intimate Apparel* and *Fabulation*

1. Zinoman, Jason. "Lynn Nottage Enters Her Flippant Period."
2. Westerfield, "Award-Winning Theatrical Team Lynn Nottage, Kate Whoriskey Discuss Their Successes."
3. Nottage, *Intimate Apparel*, 7.
4. Nottage, *Intimate Apparel*, 9.
5. Jones, *Labor of Love and Labor of Sorrow*, 134.
6. Welter, "The Cult of True Womanhood: 1820–1860," 152.
7. Kendall, *Hood Feminism*, 3.
8. Kendall, *Hood Feminism*, 4.
9. Nottage, *Intimate Apparel*, 9–10.
10. Nottage, *Intimate Apparel*, 11.
11. Nottage, *Intimate Apparel*, 39.
12. Nottage, *Intimate Apparel*, 11.
13. Nottage, *Intimate Apparel*, 39.
14. Nottage, *Intimate Apparel*, 39.
15. Nottage, *Intimate Apparel*, 39.
16. Watkins Harper, Frances Ellen, *A Brighter Coming Day*, 105.
17. Nottage, *Intimate Apparel*, 44.
18. Nottage, *Intimate Apparel*, 49.
19. Nottage, *Intimate Apparel*, 48.
20. Nottage, *Intimate Apparel*, 64.
21. Nottage, *Intimate Apparel*, 67.
22. Nottage, *Intimate Apparel*, 19.
23. Nottage, *Intimate Apparel*, 19.
24. Nottage, *Intimate Apparel*, 20.
25. Nottage, *Intimate Apparel*, 57.
26. Nottage, *Intimate Apparel*, 72.
27. Nottage, *Fabulation*, 186.
28. Nottage, *Fabulation*, 86–87.
29. Nottage, *Fabulation*, 133.
30. Chopin, *The Awakening*.
31. Nottage, *Fabulation*, 86.
32. Nottage, *Fabulation*, 88.
33. Kendall, *Hood Feminism*, 96.
34. Nottage, *Fabulation*, 85.
35. Harris-Perry, *Sister Citizen*, 184.
36. Nottage, *Fabulation*, 124.
37. Hill Collins, *Black Feminist Thought*, 88.

38. Hill Collins, *Black Feminist Thought*, 86.
39. Harris-Perry, *Sister Citizen*, 29.
40. Beal, "Double Jeopardy: To Be Black and Female," 175.

Chapter 6: Sexual Trauma and Survival in *Ruined*

1. Goodman Theatre, "A world premiere and Goodman Theatre commission." https://www.goodmantheatre.org/show/ruined/.
2. Blank, "PHOTO CALL: Lynn Nottage's *Ruined* at Manhattan Theatre Club."
3. Gener, "In Defense of *Ruined*," 118.
4. The Center for Preventive Action, "Conflict in the Democratic Republic of Congo."
5. Brownmiller, *Against Our Will*, 8.
6. Meger, "Rape in Contemporary Warfare," 101–2.
7. Meger, "Rape in Contemporary Warfare," 103.
8. Alison, "Wartime Sexual Violence," 77.
9. Brantley, "War's Terrors, Through a Brothel Window."
10. Nolen, "Not Women Anymore."
11. Nottage, *Ruined*, 12.
12. Gener, "In Defense of *Ruined*," 122.
13. Nottage, *Ruined*, 36.
14. Albutt et al., "Stigmatisation and Rejection of Survivors of Sexual Violence in Eastern Democratic Republic of the Congo," 220.
15. Nottage, *Ruined*, 34.
16. Nottage, *Ruined*, 34.
17. Nottage, *Ruined*, 37.
18. Nottage, *Ruined*, 28.
19. Nottage, *Ruined*, 68.
20. Friedman, "The Gendered Terrain in Contemporary Theatre of War by Women," 598.
21. Nottage, *Ruined*, 70.
22. Nottage, *Ruined*, 94.
23. Nottage, *Ruined*, 33.
24. Fox, "A Different Integration," 8.
25. Nottage, *Ruined*, 82–83.
26. Nottage, *Ruined*, 86.
27. Jill Dolan, *The Feminist Spectator.*
28. Nottage, *Ruined*, 91.
29. Nottage, *Ruined*, 100.
30. Jill Dolan, *The Feminist Spectator*.
31. Soloski, "Lynn Nottage's Ruined: A Worthy Pulitzer Prizewinner?"

Chapter 7: Humanizing Performers in *By the Way, Meet Vera Stark*

1. CUNYTV, "Women in Theatre: Lynn Nottage."
2. Brantley, Ben. "A Black Actress Trying to Rise Above a Maid."

3. Nottage, *By the Way*, vi.
4. Regester, *African American Actresses*, 2.
5. Fain, *Black Hollywood*, 30.
6. Fain, *Black Hollywood*, 33.
7. Fain, *Black Hollywood*, 30.
8. Nottage, *By the Way*, 23.
9. Courtney, *Hollywood Fantasies of Miscegenation*, 104.
10. Erigha, *The Hollywood Jim Crow*, 37.
11. Young, "Vera Stark at the Crossroads of History," 118.
12. Nottage, *By the Way*, 24.
13. Nottage, *By the Way*, 24–25.
14. hooks, *Ain't I a Woman*, 84.
15. hooks, *Ain't I a Woman*, 84.
16. Nottage, *By the Way*, 46.
17. Nottage, *By the Way*, 49.
18. Nottage, *By the Way*, 50.
19. Young, Vera Stark at the Crossroads of History," 114.
20. Nottage, *By the Way*, 51–52.
21. Nottage, *By the Way*, 46.
22. Nottage, *By the Way*, 47.
23. Nottage, *By the Way*, 56.
24. Nottage, *By the Way*, 62.
25. Diggs Colbert, "Playing the Help, Playing the Slave," 413–14.
26. Diggs Colbert, "Playing the Help, Playing the Slave," 413.
27. Nottage, *By the Way*, 63.
28. Diggs Colbert, "Playing the Help, Playing the Slave,"402.
29. Walker, "Zora Neale Hurston: A Cautionary Tale and a Partisan View," 86–87.
30. Nottage, *By the Way*, 91–92.
31. Walker, "Zora Neale Hurston: A Cautionary Tale and a Partisan View," 92.

Chapter 8: Anticipating the Political Divide in *Sweat*

1. Clement, "What Happened When the Cast of *Sweat* Brought the Play to the City that Inspired It."
2. Crompton, "Playwright Lynn Nottage."
3. Duggan, "A Short History of the Great Recession."
4. Tavernise, "Reading, Pa., Knew It Was Poor. Now It Knows Just How Poor."
5. Nottage, *This Is Reading*.
6. Conley, *Donald Trump and American Populism*, 159.
7. Nottage, *Sweat*, 20.
8. Nottage, *Sweat*, 22.
9. Nottage, *Sweat*, 56.
10. Nottage, *Sweat*, 56–57.
11. Phillips, "Slippery Borders and Mythic Spaces," 135.
12. Nottage, *Sweat*, 51.

13. Nottage, *Sweat*, 74–75.

14. Nottage, *Sweat*, 78.

15. Andrews, "*Sweat*: A Play for Our Times," 93.

16. Weinert-Kendt, "How Lynn Nottage, Inveterate Wanderer, Found Her Way to Reading and 'Sweat.'"

17. Nottage, *Sweat*, 45–48.

18. Haney-Lopez, *Dog Whistle Politics*, ix.

19. Burrell, "Postindustrial Futurities in Contemporary Black Feminist Theater," 66.

20. Nottage, *Sweat*, 31.

21. Clark, "How White Supremacy Returned to Mainstream Politics."

22. Nottage, *Sweat*, 90.

23. Schulman, "The First Theatrical Landmark of the Trump Era."

Chapter 9: The Question of Values in *Mlima's Tale*

1. Clement, "The Verdict."

2. Walker, "Rethinking Ivory: Why Trade in Tusks Won't Go Away," 96.

3. Bigelow, *The Last Days.*

4. Bigelow, *The Last Days.*

5. Tabor, "The Ivory Highway."

6. Brantley, "Review: An Elephant's Ghost Stalks the World in 'Mlima's Tale'"

7. Shapiro, "Pulitzer Prize-Winning Playwright Lynn Nottage on Her New Play, the Browning of America and Animal Rights."

8. Billingslea-Brown, *Crossing Borders through Folklore: African American Women's Fiction and Art*, 2.

9. Nottage, *Mlima's Tale*, 79.

10. Nottage, *Mlima's Tale*, 7.

11. Nottage, *Mlima's Tale*, 7

12. Nottage, *Mlima's Tale*, 7.

13. Nottage, *Mlima's Tale*, 14.

14. Nottage, *Mlima's Tale*, 13.

15. Nottage, *Mlima's Tale*, 26.

16. Nottage, *Mlima's Tale*, 32.

17. Nottage, *Mlima's Tale*, 40.

18. Nottage, *Mlima's Tale*, 40.

19. Nottage, *Mlima's Tale*, 44–45.

20. Nottage, *Mlima's Tale*, 49.

21. Nottage, *Mlima's Tale*, 61.

22. Nottage, *Mlima's Tale*, 53.

23. Nottage, *Mlima's Tale*, 53.

24. Archie et al., *The Amboseli Elephants: A Long-Term Perspective on a Long-Lived Mammal*, 239.

25. Nottage, *Mlima's Tale*, 68.

26. Nottage, *Mlima's Tale*, 71.

27. Nottage, *Mlima's Tale*, 73.

Conclusion: The Future Is Nottage and Elusive Justice in *Clyde's*

1. Paulson, "Lynn Nottage's 'Clyde's' Is the Most-Staged Play in America."
2. Bovard, "Review: World Premiere of Lynn Nottage's Comedy FLOYD'S at the Guthrie."
3. Alexander, *The New Jim Crow*, 71.
4. Nottage, *Clyde's*, 3.
5. Paulson, "Lynn Nottage's 'Clyde's' Is the Most-Staged Play in America."
6. Davis, *Are Prisons Obsolete?* 9.

WORKS CITED

Works by Lynn Nottage

By the Way, Meet Vera Stark. New York: Theatre Communications Group, 2013.

Clyde's. Unpublished manuscript, February 8, 2022, typescript.

Crumbs from the Table of Joy. *Crumbs from the Table of Joy and Other Plays*. New York: Theatre Communications Group, 2004, 1–88.

Fabulation, or the Re-education of Undine. In *Intimate Apparel/Fabulation: Two Plays*, New York: Theatre Communications Group, 2006, 75–140.

Intimate Apparel. In *Intimate Apparel/Fabulation: Two Plays*. New York: Theatre Communications Group, 2006, 1–74.

Las Meninas. In *Crumbs from the Table of Joy and Other Plays*. New York: Theatre Communications Group, 2004, 245–324.

Mlima's Tale. New York: Theatre Communications Group, 2021.

Mud, River, Stone. In *Crumbs from the Table of Joy and Other Plays*. New York: Theatre Communications Group, 2004, 163–243.

POOF! In *Crumbs from the Table of Joy and Other Plays*. New York: Theatre Communications Group, 2004, 90–103.

Por'Knockers. In *Crumbs from the Table of Joy and Other Plays*. New York: Theatre Communications Group, 2004, 105–62.

Ruined. New York: Theatre Communications Group, 2009.

Sweat. New York: Theatre Communications Group, 2017.

This Is Reading, accessed July 25, 2022, http://www.lynnnottage.com/this-is-reading.html.

Secondary Sources

Albutt, Katherine, Jocelyn Kelly, Justin Kabanga, and Michael VanRooyen. "Stigmatisation and Rejection of Survivors of Sexual Violence in Eastern Democratic Republic of the Congo," *Disasters* 41, no. 2 (April 2017): 211–27.

Alexander, Michelle. *The New Jim Crow*. New York: New Press, 2010.

Alison, Miranda. "Wartime Sexual Violence: Women's Human Rights and Questions of Masculinity," *Review of International Studies* 33, no. 1 (January 2007): 75–90.

Andrews, Beverly. "*Sweat*: A Play for Our Times." *New African* 598 (October 2019): 92–94.

Beal, Frances M. "Double Jeopardy: To Be Black and Female." *Meridians* 8, no. 2 (2008): 166–76. http://www.jstor.org/stable/40338758.

Berger, John. *The Success and Failure of Picasso*. London: Vintage, 1980.

Berlin, Ira. *The Making of African America: The Four Great Migrations*. New York: Viking, 2010.

Bigelow, Kathryn. "Last Days Film," on YouTube, December 7, 2014. Short film, 3:18. https://www.youtube.com/watch?v=5gQujyNDp98.

Billingslea-Brown, Alma Jean. *Crossing Borders through Folklore: African American Women's Fiction and Art*. Columbia: University of Missouri Press, 1999.

Blank, Matthew. "PHOTO CALL: Lynn Nottage's *Ruined* at Manhattan Theatre Club." *Playbill*, January 29, 2009. https://playbill.com/article/.

Brantley, Ben. "A Black Actress Trying to Rise Above a Maid." *New York Times*, May 9, 2011. https://www.nytimes.com/2011/05/10/theater/reviews/.

Brantley, Ben. "Review: An Elephant's Ghost Stalks the World in 'Mlima's Tale.'" *New York Times*, April 15, 2018. https://www.nytimes.com/2018/04/15/theater/mlimas-tale review-lynn-nottage.html.

Brantley, Ben. "War's Terrors, Through a Brothel Window." *New York Times*, February 10, 2009. https://www.nytimes.com/2009/02/11/theater/reviews/11bran.html.

Brown, Emma. "Lynn Nottage's Sweat and Blood." *Interview Magazine*, December 13, 2016. https://www.interviewmagazine.com/culture/lynn-nottage-sweat.

Brownmiller, Susan. *Against Our Will: Men, Women, and Rape*. New York: Random House, 1975.

Burnham, Kenneth E. *God Comes to America: Father Divine and The Peace Mission Movement*. Boston: Lambeth Press, 1979.

Burrell, Julie. "Postindustrial Futurities in Contemporary Black Feminist Theater: Lynn Nottage's *Sweat*, Dominique Morisseau's *Skeleton Crew*, and Lisa Langford's *The Art of Longing*." *Frontiers: A Journal of Women Studies* 42, no. 1(2021): 58–91. https://doi.org/10.1353/fro.2021.0006.

Catanese, Brandi Wilkins. "Taking the Long View." *Theatre Journal* 62, no. 4 (2010): 547–51. https://doi.org/10.1353/tj.2010.a413926.

Chopin, Kate. *The Awakening*. New York: Bantam Books, 1981.

Clark, Simon. "How White Supremacy Returned to Mainstream Politics." *Center for American Progress*, July 1, 2020. https://www.americanprogress.org/article/.

Clement, Olivia. "The Verdict." *Playbill*, April 16, 2018. https://playbill.com/article/.

Clement, Olivia. "What Happened When the Cast of *Sweat* Brought the Play to the City that Inspired It." *Playbill*, March 27, 2017, https://playbill.com/article/.

Cobert, Soyica Diggs. "Playing the Help, Playing the Slave: Disrupting Racial Fantasies in Lynn Nottage's *By the Way, Meet Vera Stark*." *Modern Drama* 59, no. 4 (Winter 2016): 399–421.

"Conflict in the Democratic Republic of Congo." Center for Preventive Action, July 20, 2023 [updated February 21, 2024]. https://www.cfr.org/global-conflict-tracker/conflict/.

Conley, Richard S. *Donald Trump and American Populism*. Edinburgh, Scotland: Edinburgh University Press. 2020.

Courtney, Susan. *Hollywood Fantasies of Miscegenation*. Princeton, NJ: Princeton University Press, 2005.

Crompton, Sarah. "Playwright Lynn Nottage: 'We are a country that has lost our narrative.'" *The Guardian*, December 2, 2018. https://www.theguardian.com/stage/2018/dec/02/.

CUNYTV. "Women in Theatre: Lynn Nottage," YouTube Video, 27:03, January 8, 2011. https://youtu.be/j1–1eEY_c4E.

Davis, Angela Y. *Are Prisons Obsolete?* New York: Seven Stories Press, 2003.

De Montespan, Madame La Marquise. *Memoirs of Madame La Marquise De Montespan*. Boston: L. C. Page and Company, 1899; Project Gutenberg, September 29, 2006. https://www.gutenberg.org/files/3854/3854-h/3854-h.htm.

Dickson-Carr, Darryl. *African American Satire: The Sacredly Profane Novel*. Columbia: University of Missouri Press, 2001.

Dolan, Jill. *Ruined*, by Lynn Nottage. *The Feminist Spectator*, March 16, 2009. https://feministspectator.princeton.edu/2009/03/16/.

Duggan, Wayne. "A Short History Of The Great Recession." *Forbes*, June 21, 2023. https://www.forbes.com/advisor/investing/.

Erigha, Maryann. *The Hollywood Jim Crow*. New York: New York University Press, 2019.

Fain, Kimberly. *Black Hollywood*. Santa Barbara, CA: Praeger, 2015.

Fanon, Frantz. *The Wretched of the Earth*. New York: Grove Press, 1963.

Foucault, Michel. *The Order of Things: An Archaeology of the Human Sciences*. New York: Pantheon Books, 1970.

Fox, Ann M. "A Different Integration: Race and Disability in Early-Twentieth-Century African American Drama by Women," *Legacy* 30, no. 1 (2013): 151–71.

Fraser, Antonia. *Love and Louis XIV: The Women in the Life of the Sun King*. New York: Anchor Books, 2007.

Friedman, Sharon. "The Gendered Terrain in Contemporary Theatre of War by Women," *Theatre Journal* 62, no. 4 (December 2010): 593–610.

Gener, Randy. "In Defense of 'Ruined': 5 Elements That Shape Lynn Nottage's Masterwork," *American Theatre* 27, no. 8 (October 2010): 118–22.

Griffith, Farah Jasmine. *Who Set You Flowin? The African-American Migration Narrative*. New York: Oxford University Press, 1995.

Hall, Jacquelyn Dowd. "The Long Civil Rights Movement and the Political Uses of the Past." *The Journal of American History* 91, no. 4 (2005): 1233–63.

Haney-Lopez, Ian. *Dog Whistle Politics: How Coded Racial Appeals Have Reinvented Racism and Wrecked the Middle Class*. New York: Oxford University Press, 2014.

Harris, Laurie Lanzer. *The Great Migration North, 1910–1970*. Detroit: Omnigraphics Inc., 2012.

Harris-Perry, Melissa V. *Sister Citizen*. New Haven, CT: Yale University Press, 2011.

Hill Collins, Patricia. *Black Feminist Thought*. New York: Routledge, 2000.

hooks, bell. *Ain't I a Woman? Black Women and Feminism*. Boston: South End Press, 1982.

Hutchinson, Earl. *Blacks and Reds: Race and Class in Conflict 1919–1990*. East Lansing: Michigan State University Press, 1995.

Jones, Claudia. "An End to the Neglect of the Problems of the Negro Woman!" Tallahassee: State University Libraries of Florida, June 1949. https://palmm.digital.flvc.org/islandora/object/ucf%3A4865.

Jones, Jacqueline. *Labor of Love, Labor of Sorrow: Black Women, Work and the Family, From Slavery to the Present.* New York: Basic Books, 2010.

Juergensmeyer, Mark. *Terror in the Mind of God.* Berkeley: University of California Press. 2000.

Kamen, Henry. *Empire: How Spain Became a World Power, 1492–1763.* New York: Penguin, 2004.

Kelley, Robin D. G. *Freedom Dreams: The Black Radical Imagination.* Boston: Beacon Press, 2003.

Kendall, Mikki. *Hood Feminism.* New York: Viking, 2020.

Levi, Anthony. *Louis XIV.* New York: Carroll & Graf, 2004.

"Lynn Nottage to Students: Replace Judgment With Curiosity," Stockton University, accessed October 2, 2023. https://stockton.edu/news/2022/.

Maxwell, Dominic. "Lynn Nottage: 'There Are Not Many People Who Look Like Me Who Have Been Writing Plays for 25 Years.'" *The Times*, April 17, 2023.

Meger, Sarah. "Rape in Contemporary Warfare: The Role of Globalization in Wartime Sexual Violence," *African Conflict and Peacebuilding Review* 1, no. 1 (Spring 2011): 100–32.

Miles, Robert J. "If It's Baroque, Don't Fix It: Picasso's Exilic Resurrection of Velázquez and the (Ab)use of *Las Meninas.*" *Journal of Iberian and Latin American Studies* 7, no. 2 (2001): 173–89.

Moss, Cynthia J., Harvey Croze, and Phyllis C. Lee. *The Amboseli Elephants: A Long-Term Perspective on a Long-Lived Mammal.* Chicago: University of Chicago Press, 2011.

Nolen, Stephanie. "'Not Women Anymore: The Congo's rape survivors face pain, shame and AIDS," *Ms. Magazine*, May 7, 2005. http://www.msmagazine.com/spring2005/congo.asp.

Phillips, M. Scott. "Slippery Borders and Mythic Spaces: Race, Class, and Ressentiment in Lynn Nottage's *Sweat.*" *Theatre Symposium* 29 (2022): 133–49. https://doi.org/10.1353/tsy.2022.0011.

"Political Theatre." *Dramatist* 16, no. 4 (2014): 16–31.

Press, Steven. *Rogue Empires: Contracts and Conmen in Europe's Scramble for Africa.* Cambridge, MA: Harvard University Press, 2017.

Regester, Charlene. *African American Actresses.* Bloomington: Indiana University Press, 2010.

Rodgers, Lawrence R. *Canaan Bound: The African American Migration Novel.* Champaign: University of Illinois Press, 1997.

Rothstein, Mervin. "Round Five for a Theatrical Heavyweight," *New York Times*, April 15, 1990. https://www.nytimes.com/1990/04/15/theater/.

"Ruined." Chicago: Goodman Theatre, 2024. https://www.goodmantheatre.org/show/ruined/.

Schulman, Michael. "The First Theatrical Landmark of the Trump Era." *New Yorker*, March 27, 2017. https://www.newyorker.com/magazine/2017/03/27/.

Shannon, Sandra G. "An Interview with Lynn Nottage." In *Contemporary African American Women Playwrights*, edited by Philip C. Kolin, 194–201. New York: Routledge, 2007.

Shannon, Sandra G. "An Intimate Look at the Plays of Lynn Nottage." In *Contemporary African American Women Playwrights*, edited by Philip C. Kolin, 185–93. New York: Routledge, 2007.

Shannon, Sandra G. "A Transplant That Did Not Take: August Wilson's Views on the Great Migration." *African American Review* 31, no. 4 (1997): 659–66. https://doi.org/10.2307/3042334.

Shapiro, Eben. "Pulitzer Prize-Winning Playwright Lynn Nottage on Her New Play, the Browning of America and Animal Rights." TIME.com, May 17, 2018. https://time.com/5280436/.

Solomon, Mark. *The Cry Was Unity: Communists and African Americans 1917–1936*. Jackson: University of Mississippi Press, 1998.

Soloski, Alexis. "Lynn Nottage's Ruined: A Worthy Pulitzer Prizewinner?" *The Guardian*, April 21, 2009. https://www.theguardian.com/stage/theatreblog/2009/apr/21/.

Sommer, Elyse. "A *CurtainUp* Review: *Mud, River, Stone*." *CurtainUp*, December 17, 1997. http://www.curtainup.com/mud.html.

Stars, Courtney. "When God Drove a Cadillac: The Remarkable Story of Father Divine." *Medium*, October 7, 2019. https://medium.com/@courtneystars/.

Stockho, Thelma R. "French Paintings of the Seventeenth and Eighteenth Centuries." *Bulletin* 16, no. 1 (Summer 1981): 1–28. https://www.jstor.org/stable/40716043.

Stratton, Tari. "In Conversation: Lynn Nottage & Paula Vogel." *Dramatist* 19, no. 5 (2017): 10–19.

Tabor, Damon. "The Ivory Highway." *Men's Journal*, December 4, 2017. https://www.mensjournal.com/travel/.

Tavernise, Sabrina. "Reading, Pa., Knew It Was Poor. Now It Knows Just How Poor." *The New York Times*, September 26, 2011. https://www.nytimes.com/2011/09/27/us/.

Wallace, Michele. *Black Macho and the Myth of the Superwoman*. New York: Dial Press, 1979.

Walker, Alice. *In Search of Our Mothers' Gardens*. Orlando, FL: Harcourt Brace & Company, 1983.

Walker Alice. "Zora Neale Hurston: A Cautionary Tale and a Partisan View." In *In Search of Our Mothers' Gardens*, 83–92. Orlando, FL: Harcourt Brace & Company, 1983.

Walker, John Frederick. "Rethinking Ivory: Why Trade in Tusks Won't Go Away." *World Policy Journal* 30, no. 2 (Summer 2013): 91–100. http://www.jstor.org/stable/43290229.

Washington, Booker T. *Up From Slavery*. New York: Doubleday, 1901.

Watkins Harper, Frances Ellen. "The Two Offers." In *A Brighter Coming Day: A Frances Ellen Watkins Harper Reader*, edited by Frances Smith Foster, 105–14. New York: The Feminist Press, 1990.

Watts, Jill. *God, Harlem U.S.A.: The Father Divine Story*. Berkeley: University of California Press, 1992.

Weinert-Kendt, Rob. "How Lynn Nottage, Inveterate Wanderer, Found Her Way to Reading and 'Sweat.'" *American Theatre*, July 10, 2015. https://www.americantheatre.org/2015/07/10/.

Welter, Barbara. "The Cult of True Womanhood: 1820–1860." *American Quarterly* 18, no. 2(1966): 151–74. https://www.jstor.org/stable/2711179.

Westerfield, Joe. "Award-Winning Theatrical Team Lynn Nottage, Kate Whoriskey Discuss Their Successes." *Newsweek*, November 30, 2021. https://www.newsweek.com/.

Wilkerson, Isabel. *The Warmth of Other Suns*. New York: Vintage, 2010.

Young, Harvey. "Vera Stark at the Crossroads of History." In *A Critical Companion to Lynn Nottage*, edited by Jocelyn L. Buckner, 110–25. New York: Routledge, 2016.

Zinoman, Jason. "Lynn Nottage Enters Her Flippant Period." *New York Times*, June 13, 2004. https://www.nytimes.com/2004/06/13/theater/.

INDEX